About this Learning Guide

Shmoop Will Make You a Better Lover*
*of Literature, History, Poetry, Life...

Our lively learning guides are written by experts and educators who want to show your brain a good time. Shmoop writers come primarily from Ph.D. programs at top universities, including Stanford, Harvard, and UC Berkeley.

Want more Shmoop? We cover literature, poetry, bestsellers, music, US history, civics, biographies (and the list keeps growing). Drop by our website to see the latest.

www.shmoop.com

Table of Contents

Introduction

In a Nutshell

In 2008 *Lolita* turned 50 – *Lolita* the novel, that is, not Lolita the nymphet. The book still has the power to enflame passions. In Marion County, Florida a few years back, one citizen insisted that the book be shelved in the "adults only" section of the library. That didn't happen (by a vote 3-2 in favor of keeping it available to all), but as one critic has said, "[W]e all know that this novel heads every prude's list and has had to fight for its life from the very beginning" (source: James Kincaid, "Lolita at Middle Age").

Some snippets of contemporary reviews of the novel give you an idea or its reception:

- "Most readers will probably become bored [...] at times downright sickened" (*The Providence Journal*).
- "[T]his book is "distilled sewage" (*The New York World Telegraph*).
- *Lolita* is "pornography" (*The Chicago Tribune*).

Among the most well-known reviews is one from the more forward-thinking *New York Times*, whose reviewer, Orville Prescott, called the book "repulsive" with a refined depravity that makes for "highbrow pornography." More importantly, Prescott angrily asserts: "Part of its theoretical comedy probably lies in the fact that the child, Lolita, turns out to be just as corrupt as Humbert – a notion that does not strike one as notably funny" (source).

OK, so the book has offended a lot of people. Isn't that reason enough to read how Humbert Humbert's lust for his step-daughter serves as an effort to get over the loss of his childhood girlfriend?

The first American edition appeared in 1958 (after four American publishers rejected it), but in 1955 a version was published by Olympia Press, a French publisher of erotica. Despite all of this rejection and outrage, people love it – over 50 million copies have sold since the book's publication in 1958. It was the first book since *Gone with the Wind* to sell 100,000 copies in its first three weeks. The highly reputable Modern Library named *Lolita* the fourth-greatest English-language book of the twentieth century, right behind *The Great Gatsby*, *A Portrait of an Artist as a Young Man*, and *Ulysses*. The book was banned as obscene in France (France!) and England from 1955-1959, as well as Argentina (1959), New Zealand (1960), and South Africa (1974-1982). It has never been banned in the United States, though it puts a lot of knickers in a twist.

During his life, Vladimir Nabokov published eighteen novels, eight books of short stories, seven books of poetry, and nine plays – none nearly so attention getting as *Lolita*. Amazingly, English

was not even his first language – Russian was. Addressing the, well, sensitive material in a 1962 BBC interview, Nabokov said, *Lolita* "was my most difficult book – the book that treated of a theme which was so distant, so remote, from my own emotional life that it gave me a special pleasure to use my combinational talent to make it real" (source). Despite this clear position, critics and readers *still* like to think Nabokov is a pervert just for *writing* the book. Who could write a story *this* real without having *those* feelings?

Nabokov and his wife, Véra (to whom the book is dedicated) traveled around the United States on butterfly hunting trips quite a bit, which makes his descriptions of 1950s America incredibly vivid. On these trips, Nabokov became very familiar with American mass culture, finding it both mesmerizing and repulsive. He wrote *Lolita* as he traveled though Colorado, Wyoming, Arizona, and Oregon, copying the manuscript in longhand. In a revealing epilogue to the book, included in all versions since 1956, Nabokov addresses his critics. He is attracted to taboo, he tells us, and despite all assumptions to the contrary, there is no "moral of the story" in *Lolita*. Nabokov just wants you to enjoy *Lolita*.

Why Should I Care?

We could tell you to care about *Lolita* because it is a classic of twentieth-century American fiction – or because it has been banned and scorned by so many librarians, literary critics, and judges. But the real reason you should care about *Lolita* is that the character of 'tween Lolita has become an icon and inspiration in popular culture. Almost disturbingly so.

Lolita isn't just a character in a Nabokov novel or a famous nymphet; Lolita has been claimed by fashionistas and fetishists, transformed into the embodiment of knee-sock and mini-plaid skirt wearing promiscuous school girl. Lolita has inspired everything from the subculture of "Gothic Lolita," a popular Japanese style that embraces Rococo and Victorian clothing types, to "Sweet Lolita," "Classic Lolita," and "Punk Lolita."

The most well known in America is the plain old Lolita-influenced style. The sexy 'tween image of a younger Britney Spears or Miley Cyrus owes a big debt to *Lolita*, for good or ill. Popular culture seems to love the image of young sexy girls. Skin tight miniskirts for 11-year-olds? A "hottie" t-shirt for a fifth-grader? Are these things empowering or exploitative? A book called *The Lolita Effect* (2008) by M. Gigi Durham is dedicated to this subject, explaining that the very word "Lolita" is now shorthand for an overly sexualized, provocative adolescent.

What's interesting about this cultural phenomenon is that it makes no mention of Humbert, the middle-aged man whose exploitative urges ruin young Lolita's life.

Summary

Book Summary

John Ray, Jr., Ph.D. writes a Foreword to Humbert's memoir, *Lolita, or the Confessions of a White, Widowed Male*. Ray explains that Humbert died in jail in 1952, right before he was set to go to trial.

Humbert's memoir begins by describing his childhood in the Riviera, where his father owns a luxury hotel. Humbert has many experiences, chief among them, his mother is struck by lightening. But, more prominently, he falls in love (and deep lust) with a "nymphet" girl-child named Annabel Leigh, who is at the hotel on vacation with her parents. Thwarted consummation of his sexual urges creates a life-long obsession with nymphets.

Humbert receives an education in France and England. He marries Valeria, who ends up leaving him for a Russian cab driver. Receiving an inheritance from an uncle, Humbert moves to the United States. Humbert spends time writing and dipping in and out of mental institutes. He finally decides to settle down in Ramsdale, where he moves in with the widow Charlotte Haze and her nymphet daughter, Lolita.

Humbert fixates on Lolita while barely tolerating her vulgar, middlebrow mother. Disgusted with her daughter's bratty behavior, Charlotte packs Lolita off to Camp Q and issues Humbert an ultimatum: love me or leave me. To stay in Lolita's life, Humbert marries Charlotte. An hysterical Charlotte is hit by a car after reading Humbert's diary and discovering his dark lust for her daughter and deep hatred of her.

Humbert picks up Lolita at Camp Q and spirits her off to The Enchanted Hunters hotel. They have sex, which, according to Humbert, she initiates. A stranger expresses to Humbert his fascination with Lolita; Humbert has no idea who he is, plus it's dark so he can't see him.

Humbert and Lolita spend a year driving all over the United States. Lolita starts getting a little bratty, challenging Humbert's sexual demands; he threatens to send her to an orphanage or reform school if she doesn't straighten up. He also feeds her constant craving for souvenirs, Hollywood movies, and pop cultural junk.

Humbert and Lolita move to Beardsley. He gets a job teaching and she goes to the Beardsley School for girls, run by Mrs. Pratt. Lolita takes up an interest in boys, but is even more eager to join the school play, *The Enchanted Hunters*. Trying to keep her happy, Humbert consents.

Humbert starts getting nervous about Lolita's fidelity to him, so they go on a trip. This time she plans the itinerary. Along the road, they are shadowed by a man in a red car who resembles

Humbert's Uncle Trapp.

Lolita becomes sick and must go into the hospital. While Humbert is back at the motel, Lolita leaves with a strange man. Humbert begins his obsessed hunt for Lolita, tracing back through every motel they visited. He spends years looking for her, during which time he hooks up with a kind-hearted alcoholic named Rita.

Humbert receives a letter from Lolita; he tracks her down to a shanty in Coalmont.

Humbert meets with a very pregnant Lolita, gets the story of her escape with Quilty, begs her to return to him, and gives her money from the sale of the Haze home. Now she can move to Alaska with her working-class husband, Dick.

Humbert tracks down Quilty and kills him in his family home, Pavor Manor. Driving the wrong way down the street, Humbert is arrested. In jail, he writes his memoir.

Foreword

- Humbert Humbert, author of the manuscript, originally titled the *Lolita, or the Confession of a White Widowed Male*, died in 1952 in "legal captivity" (Fore.1), though we don't know what he was there for in the first place.
- Humbert Humbert's attorney contacted the author of the Foreword and asked him to edit and publish it after Humbert's death.
- Very few changes were made to the manuscript. Though the names were changed to protect the innocent, as they say – all, that is except Lolita because her name is so integral to the story.
- If you care to do a little research in newspapers from fall of 1952, you would be able to confirm that "H.H."'s crime really occurred, though you won't find out why.
- The fate of several people is announced – for example, a Mrs. Richard F. Schiller has died in childbirth – though who all of these folks are remains unclear.
- Though the novel's subject matter is very racy, there are no "four-letter words" (Fore.4). Far from pornography, the novel teaches moral lessons.
- Reader, be warned: the novel's narrator is a monster but a darned good writer and an honest one at that.
- We have a lot to learn from the story, particularly about being more attentive guardians of innocent children.

Book 1, Chapter 1

- Humbert describes the pleasure he derives from saying Lolita's name and cites its many variations – Dolores, Lo, Dolly.

- Before Lolita, he had another "girl-child" (1.1.2) lover.
- Humbert refers to himself as a murderer with a good prose style.
- He refers to the reader as "Ladies and gentlemen of the jury" (1.1.4), preparing us to hear his dark tale.

Book 1, Chapter 2

- Humbert was born in Paris in 1910, a mixture of Swiss, French, and Austrian descent.
- His father owned a luxury hotel on the Riviera, where he was raised with the help of an aunt, Sybil.
- His beautiful mother met her death in an accident, which he describes in two parenthetical words: "(picnic, lightning)" (1.2.1).
- The hotel was a lovely place to grow up.
- Humbert attended an English day school near the hotel.
- Then he met Annabel. Before her, his sexual experiences involved French movies and enjoying some French book he stole from the hotel library.
- So back to Annabel. When he met her, Humbert was alone, with no one to consult about matters of sex, as his father was off on a trip.

Book 1, Chapter 3

- Humbert's memory of Annabel is vague as his post-Lolita mind set blurs his visual recollection of his first love.
- Annabel's parents were seriously uptight.
- Humbert and Annabel enjoyed discussing what they would do as grown-ups.
- Hooking up was no easy task, as Annabel's parents would barely let her out of their sight.
- They enjoyed sexual encounters on the sly, such as holding hands under the sand at the beach. This lack of true action drove them both nuts.
- Humbert recalls finding an old photograph in which Annabel appears, but is not looking at the camera.
- Directly after the photograph was taken, Humbert and Annabel made another thwarted attempt to hook up. Four months later she died of typhus on the island of Corfu.

Book 1, Chapter 4

- Humbert muses whether Annabel caused the dark desires of his adult life or presented just

the first example of it. He believes, as he explains it, that Lolita began with Annabel.

- Annabel's death made the failure to consummate even worse. Their love went both ways; Lolita never loved him as Annabel did.
- Humbert returns to the subject of his "first tryst" (1.4.3) with Annabel. Looks like they went to second base (or something like that).
- He recalls her lovely scent and many of the other visual and tactile pleasures of the encounter. Her spell was broken 24 years later when he met Lolita.

Book 1, Chapter 5

- Humbert recounts his more general relations to women during his college years.
- He considered getting a degree in psychiatry but then switched to English literature, which he studied in Paris.
- He begins publishing and finds a teaching job.
- Humbert introduces and details the term "nymphet" (1.5.5); nymphets are girls between 9 and 14 and don't have to be good looking. To discern a nymphet is also a skill – you must yourself be, as he says, an "artist and a madman" (1.5.6).
- There must be a gap of at least ten years between the man and his nymphet. Thus, by definition, Annabel is not one but his love for her fueled his love of nymphets.
- Living in Europe, Humbert had relations with many women, all of whom are substitutes and many of whom are prostitutes; taboo prevents him from being with a girl of twelve, but he spends plenty of time staring at them in parks.
- Humbert recounts many examples from literature and history in which poets and leaders loved much younger girls.
- He "tried hard to be good" (1.5.19), spending many days sitting on a park bench ogling nymphets but restraining himself.

Book 1, Chapter 6

- Humbert considers whether his unconsummated lust affected the nymphets he so coveted. He also wonders what became of them as grown up women.
- He recalls his affair with "a young whore" (1.6.4) named Monique; it ends when she grows out of her nymphet cuteness.
- On his quest for other nymphets he has an unpleasant run-in that ends when he pays the prostitute but does not have sex with her.

Book 1, Chapter 7

- Humbert decides that marriage would be a good smokescreen for his perversion. Plus, having a wife to do everything for you would be nice.
- He marries Valeria, the daughter of a Polish doctor.
- Humbert reiterates that he is "an exceptionally handsome male" (7.1) but not always wise in matters of sex.

Book 1, Chapter 8

- Though Valeria was not a nymphet (too old), she at least reminded him of one with her girlish ways and cutesy hairdo.
- Soon after they are married, Humbert watches her vague nymphet resemblance fade. They remain married from 1935-1939.
- When an uncle dies in 1939, Humbert receives a small inheritance, but it requires that he move to America to look after the uncle's business.
- Valeria confesses that she is having an affair – with the taxi driver whose cab they are riding in.
- Humbert is enraged – as a husband would be – but also bitter because he had restrained himself from nymphets all of those years. He considers all sorts of violent reactions.
- They all three go back to the apartment and she packs her bags.
- Humbert later finds out that Valeria moved to Pasadena, California, where she dies in childbirth in 1945.
- Humbert reports what books he reads in the prison library. He transcribes one page from a book called *Who's Who in the Limelight* , with entries on "Quilty, Clare" and "Quine, Dolores." Since one of Lolita's names was Dolores, he gets excited by the very sight of that name on a page, even though it's not her.
- He engages in some word play "Guilty of killing Quilty" (1.8.4) and so forth, none of which makes sense to the reader, and ends by lamenting that all he has left is "words to play with" (1.8.4).

Book 1, Chapter 9

- Humbert divorces and moves to the United States where he edits perfume ads and continues work on his "comparative history of French literature for English-speaking students" (1.9.1).
- He has a breakdown and goes to a sanatorium for more than a year, returns to work, re-enters the sanatorium.

- He participates in an exploratory voyage to the Arctic, during which he is supposed to make observations about the psychological state of his colleagues. He doesn't enjoy the job because "Nymphets do not occur in polar regions" (1.9.3).
- Upon his return, Humbert suffers another breakdown and enters the sanatorium a third time. Mocking the psychoanalysts helps pass the time though, as he loves outsmarting and misleading them about the causes and symptoms of his disorder. He is particularly amused that they think he is "potentially homosexual" (1.9.5).

Book 1, Chapter 10

- Back on the streets, Humbert decides that the New England countryside would be a good place to settle down.
- An opportunity to live with a Mr. McCoo, the cousin of a former employee, appeals to him because McCoo has a twelve-year-old daughter. But their house burns down. Still, Mr. McCoo reports, "a friend of his wife's, a grand person, Mrs. Haze of 342 Lawn Street" (1.10.3) offers to take Humbert in.
- Living in Ramsdale is not Humbert's idea of a good time and the outside appearance of the Haze house horrifies him. Inside is just as bad, with its foreign bric-a-brac, fake French masterpieces, and vulgar aspirations to sophistication.
- Enter Charlotte Haze – wagging cigarette, sandals, slacks – not unattractive but a living cliché of the suburban American middle-aged woman. In a word: banal.
- A tour of the house reveals the real appeal: Charlotte's twelve-year-old daughter, Dolores, who bears an uncanny resemblance to Annabel, his "Riviera love" (1.10.11).
- That's it – he's moving in – or as he puts it: "I find it most difficult to express with adequate force that flash, that shiver, that impact of passionate recognition" (1.10.13).
- Humbert concludes the discussion by addressing his "judges" (his readers), knowing they will think his desires are those of a madman.

Book 1, Chapter 11

- From prison, Humbert muses over diary entries from 1947, his early encounters with Dolores (a.k.a. Lolita). Though the diary itself was destroyed, he vividly remembers what he recorded in it.
- Some of his recollections include detailed descriptions of what Dolores wore one day as she removed clothes from the clothesline – her skin, her ankle-bone – he doesn't miss a thing.
- Memories of her walk and slangy speech still thrill him. He knows it is risky to record these illicit feelings in his journal, but he just can't help it! (Restraint is not his strong suit.)
- Erotic images of Dolores are often ruined by the presence of Charlotte – "mother Haze," he

snidely dubs her – whom Humbert accepts as the high cost of being near the nymphet. The contrast between mother and daughter is almost too much to bear. He has fantasies about killing "mother Haze."

Book 1, Chapter 12

- Humbert thinks up ways to gratify himself without violating Lolita's chastity.
- Plans to go to Hourglass Lake with Lolita and Mrs. Haze must constantly be rescheduled, much to Humbert's irritation. The fact that one of Lolita's pals will be joining them when they do go irks him even more.
- Humbert lapses into thoughts of how fate (what he calls McFate) brought him and Lolita together – thanks to some old woman named Miss Phalen breaking her hip.

Book 1, Chapter 13

- Just when they think the trip to the lake will happen, it doesn't. Angry Lolita refuses to go to church and so stays home with Humbert.
- Humbert gets really cozy with his reader here, wanting to make sure that we don't think that he's a pervert because of the story he is about to tell us. As he often does, Humbert lays out the events like he is describing a scene in a movie.
- This is what he tells us:
- He and Lolita are sitting on the couch engaging in some highly symbolic extended flirtation involving an apple. While Lolita moves around on the couch fighting over a magazine with Humbert, he derives secret pleasure from her body's movements near his.
- Humbert describes his private climax in highly poetic terms. Lolita doesn't even appear to notice that he has just had achieved a "euphoria of release" (1.13.12), and trots off in her silly way.

Book 1, Chapter 14

- Humbert congratulates himself for achieving sexual satisfaction without becoming a criminal pervert and without her knowing. He yearns to repeat the act – but her purity is important too and part of the attraction in the first place.
- At dinner that night Charlotte announces that Lolita will be going off to camp for two months. Shocked, Humbert pretends he has a toothache, so Charlotte recommends their neighbor who is a dentist: Dr. Ivor Quilty. "Uncle or cousin," she says, "I think, of the

playwright" (1.14.7).

Book 1, Chapter 15

- While Lolita pouts in her room and reads comic books, Charlotte talks about what a naughty girl she is to Humbert. Lolita's problem is, Charlotte explains, she thinks she's a starlet.
- Charlotte has told Lolita that Humbert wants Lolita off at camp too, so now the nymphet thinks he's a traitor.
- Humbert confirms that he had, at that point, "fallen in love with Lolita forever" (1.15.3) and would continue to love her even though she was about to turn thirteen. He then goes into a detailed description of her physical qualities (and if you use a dictionary you will discover what a sicko he really is).
- Humbert worries that other predators at "Camp Q" will get at Lolita at compromise her nymphet status.
- Some gratification is achieved when Lolita gives Humbert a big kiss on the mouth when she goes off to camp.

Book 1, Chapter 16

- The kiss is almost too much for Humbert to bear, but he is shocked to his senses when Louise, the maid, hands him a love letter from Charlotte. The letter is confession-style, complete with bad French phrases and sentimental descriptions of how long she has loved him; she commands that he leave immediately if he does not feel the same.
- He also finds out that Lolita had a little brother who died at age two, when Lolita was four.
- He throws the letter in the toilet.
- Wandering in the house feeling disgust about the letter, Humbert finds himself in Lolita's room. Pinned to her wall is an ad featuring a vaguely handsome man. Humbert notices that Lolita wrote "H.H." next to it with an arrow. Next to the ad is a picture of a playwright smoking a Drome cigarette.

Book 1, Chapter 17

- Humbert plays with the idea of marrying Charlotte to stay near Lolita, though such a notion is torture to him.
- His thoughts turn to sleeping medication. He indulges the idea of drugging them both so

that he can have his way with Lolita while Charlotte is out cold.

- He tries to reach Charlotte at the camp but instead gets Lolita on the phone. He tells her he plans to marry her mother. Her response: "Gee, that's swell" (1.17.7).
- As he awaits the arrival of Charlotte's blue sedan, Humbert begins drinking heavily.

Book 1, Chapter 18

- Wedding plans begin, during which time Charlotte begins to quiz Humbert on his loyalties to God. Apparently his faith is important because she threatens to kill herself if he is not a good Christian.
- Charlotte immediately takes to the idea of being Humbert's wife, acting like a refined lady and a domestic goddess. She also really looks like she is in love, which makes her a little bit pretty to him. When he feels pangs of disgust toward Charlotte, he reminds himself of his wife's biological proximity to Lolita.
- Charlotte also goes on a nesting tear, fixing up everything in the house from sofa to blinds and reading books with titles like *Your Home is You* (1.18.8).
- Humbert and Charlotte do some socializing with the Farlows – John and Jean. John handles "some of Charlotte's [legal] affairs" (1.18.9). Jean is John's young wife and cousin with pointy breasts and red lips. Their niece, Rosaline, attends school with Lolita.
- One day, John Farlow shows Humbert how to use a gun.

Book 1, Chapter 19

- Humbert warns us that a bad accident is going to happen, but first a few words about the new Mrs. Humbert. For one, she is jealous, possessive, and nosy. She wants all the details of Humbert's past affairs, so he makes up some things to make her happy. Charlotte thrills at the stories and reciprocates by providing lurid details of her many erotic experiences.
- Humbert finds Charlotte's stories about as interesting as her autopsy would be. Unfortunately she does not discuss Lolita nearly enough – and her dislike of her own daughter annoys him.
- She does mention having a baby with Humbert, an idea that not surprisingly revolts him. He much prefers the "incestuous thrill" (19.3) of being Lolita's daddy.

Book 1, Chapter 20

- To escape the summer heat, Humbert and Charlotte spend a lot of time at Hourglass Lake.

Charlotte complains that she wants to fire Louise and get a "real trained" German servant. She also explains that she wants to dispatch Lolita to Beardsley College, a boarding school, straight from camp!

- Needless to say, Humbert is seized by violent emotions – with classic hand wringing and an urge to throttle Charlotte. He knows that Charlotte, at once stupid and shrewd, would become suspicious if he protested sending Lolita off to school. He daydreams about murdering Charlotte right then and there at the lake, imagining in detail how the ugly scene would go down. He decides it's not such a hot idea.
- After working on a painting a ways up from the lake, Jean Farlow joins them on the beach. She begins talking about Ivor Quilty and his nephew, but her husband walks up and interrupts her.

Book 1, Chapter 21

- Charlotte charges on, busying herself by working on the house, yammering on the phone, and mailing letters.
- One night, Charlotte announces that she has planned a trip to England. Humbert resists by recourse to a lecture about how married couples make decisions together. He adds that he is "allergic to Europe" (1.21.8) because of bad memories from the place. Charlotte begs for forgiveness and wants to make love immediately.
- Humbert retreats to his den where he pretends to get work done.
- Meddlesome Charlotte can't stand to leave him alone. One day she finds his desk locked, which makes her very suspicious. She mentions going to a hotel called The Enchanted Hunters for a romantic getaway. Humbert is concerned that the desk may not be well hidden enough.

Book 1, Chapter 22

- News comes that Lolita cannot begin boarding school until January, so Humbert goes to the doctor to get his sleeping pills so he can drug her and take advantage of her. He really plays up his insomnia so that the doctor gives him something strong.
- He also realizes that in his eagerness he may be getting sloppy as he accidentally mentions to the doctor that he had been in a sanatorium.
- Pleased with his acquisition of the pills, Humbert returns home.
- Here's where it gets ugly: Charlotte got into his desk and read his letters. A sample: "The Haze woman, the big bitch, the old cat, the obnoxious mamma" (1.22.5). She not only knows what a cow he thinks she is, but also that he lusts after Lolita. Not good. She also she has written some letters – perhaps to Lolita, telling her of these sordid revelations – which she plans to mail immediately.

- A desperate Humbert scrambles by explaining that they are notes for novel and that she is crazy. Humbert retreats to a kitchen for a stiff drink.
- Just then a man calls on the phone and tells Humbert that Charlotte has been hit by a car. Now Humbert is really addled because he just left her in the living room. He returns and realizes that she really is gone.

Book 1, Chapter 23

- Running outside, Humbert finds a chaotic scene. In her haste to mail some letters, Charlotte tripped and fell in front of a moving car that was itself trying to avoid hitting a dog.
- Humbert acts fast, gathering up the unmailed incriminating letters. In a whirl of anxiety, he sees himself as he imagines others seeing him: "The widower, a man of exceptional self-control, neither wept nor raved" (23.2).
- The Farlows come to console him. Humbert does a lot of drinking and reads the letters: one to a reform school, one to Lolita, and one to him.
- Humbert concocts a story for the Farlows about how he and Charlotte had an affair long ago, all of which is to imply that Lolita *just might* be his daughter so she can't be taken away from him.
- Humbert puts on a big show of bereavement and concern and convinces the Farlows not to notify Lolita at camp – he doesn't want to ruin her vacation with the news.
- Among many other "busybodies" dropping by the house is a man named Beale, who comes by to explain how he ran over Charlotte and to sell the idea that it was really her fault. Humbert thanks fate for clearing his path to Lolita and takes the man up on his offer to pay for the funeral.

Book 1, Chapter 24

- Humbert muses on how his masculine good looks and professorial charm manage to attract all kinds of women.
- Apparently Jean Farlow is no exception. As Humbert leaves to retrieve his daughter from camp, Jean "glues" a passionate kiss on his lips.

Book 1, Chapter 25

- Humbert is torn between thanking his lucky stars and recognizing the ethical problems presented by his perverse ways.

- His lust wins out, of course, and he races to Camp Q (past Lake Climax) to swoop up the newly orphaned Lolita. She's all his.
- A two-day hike prevents him from immediately seizing her and so he goes into town to indulge in a shopping spree that brings to his mind every dimension of Lolita's adolescent figure. The very act of shopping for her is an erotic experience.
- He makes a reservation at an inn that Charlotte previously mentioned, by the name of The Enchanted Hunters.

Book 1, Chapter 26

- Back to present time (remember Humbert is telling this whole story from prison): Humbert reflects upon the dismal realities of being incarcerated. He admits to being a little confused by the order of events but remains focused on the date August 15, 1947 and, of course, on Lolita.

Book 1, Chapter 27

- After a sleepless night, Humbert heads back to Camp Q. He takes in all the details as he awaits Lolita's arrival. An extended description of her every feature attends her arrival. Humbert momentarily has paternal feelings but quickly recovers his desire.
- Humbert has contrived an elaborate story about how Charlotte is in the hospital with "something abdominal" (1.27.6). An indifferent Lolita asks Humbert when he fell in love with her mother and then launches into accusations about her infidelity to him: "I've been revoltingly unfaithful to you, but it does not matter one bit, because you've stopped caring for me anyway" (1.27.23). She kisses him and he shows the will power of a saint.
- A police officer stops them and asks if they have seen a blue sedan. Humbert races off to the hotel. Between chastising him about his speeding, Lolita cajoles Humbert into admitting that they are lovers. She flirts and provokes and then calls him a "dirty man" (1.27.75) when he shows affection.
- They finally arrive at The Enchanted Hunters and check into room 342 (same number as their street address). After several high jinx, it turns out that Humbert and Lolita will have to share a double bed. Lolita is catching on to his tricks; when he insists that he is driven by paternal duty, she responds by saying, "The word is incest" (1.27.108).
- Time for dinner. They go down to the dining hall, where Lolita spots the writer Quilty (who has appeared in a Drome cigarette ad that Lolita has pinned above her bed). Humbert confuses this Quilty for the Ramsdale dentist, Quilty, the uncle of the writer.
- Humbert gives Lolita sleeping pills, which he tells her are vitamins. A drowsy Lolita tries to confess some naughty behavior at Camp Q but Humbert leaves her to pass out completely.

Book 1, Chapter 28

- This is the moment Humbert has been waiting for. He explains to the reader (whom he addresses as "Gentlewomen of the jury" (28.1) that her purity is important to him, so he will only take advantage of her while she sleeps. (Uh...)
- He wanders downstairs looking for a drink, goes to the men's room, chats with the concierge, and goes out the lobby to stand outside in the dark. The anticipation of returning to the room is overwhelming him.
- A voice out of the darkness addresses Humbert and begins asking all sorts of familiar questions about Lolita. The man's double entendres suggest that he is on to Humbert, but both play innocent.
- Walking back through the lobby, Humbert is caught by the "blinding flash" (28.24) of a camera.

Book 1, Chapter 29

- Humbert returns to the hotel room. Though dozy, Lolita is not fast asleep and begins mumbling the name Barbara to him. Humbert lays awake all night anxiously listening to the irritating noises of the hotel. Though laying next to her, he dares not make his move.
- Lolita finally wakes up at 6 am and, Humbert tells us, "by six fifteen we were technically lovers" (1.29.12), but it is she who seduces him! (Or so he says.) Lolita proves to be quite experienced – the one in control.

Book 1, Chapter 30

- Humbert describes the way he would redecorate The Enchanted Hunters if he were a painter. In his hands, the place would have murals of idealistic and romantic camp activities.

Book 1, Chapter 31

- Humbert digresses into a discussion of a Roman law that allowed girls to marry at twelve. He explains that the law was adopted by some states in the US.
- He also tells us that he was not Lolita's first lover.

Book 1, Chapter 32

- Lolita details all of her erotic experiences for Humbert, among them lesbian liaisons at camp, which Humbert calls "sapphic diversions" (1.32.13). She had several hook-ups at Camp Q, taking turns with her friend Barbara at having sex with the camp mistress's son, Charlie Holmes.
- Lolita tries on all of the cute outfits Humbert bought for her. As they prepare to check out of the hotel, he warns Lolita not to talk to strangers.
- Humbert begins expressing paranoia. He resents some man staring at Lolita; he feels pangs of guilt for hurting her; he feels lust as he drives.
- Lolita teases Humbert: "You revolting creature. I was a daisy-fresh girl and look what you've done to me. I ought to call the police and tell them you raped me. Oh, you dirty, dirty old man" (1.32.33).
- Lolita wants to call her mother, but Humbert announces that she is dead.

Book 1, Chapter 33

- In Lepingville, Humbert does some major impulse shopping to appease Lolita. He is now all she has.

Book 2, Chapter 1

- They begin their long journey around the United States. Humbert goes into great detail about the motels they stay in; all of the Americana is fascinating to him: "Sunset Motels, U-Beam Cottages, Hillcrest Courts, Pine View Courts, Mountain View Courts" (2.1.3). Lolita's favorites are the "Colonial" Inns, but they usually stay in ordinary motor courts.
- Humbert realizes a few things about Lolita: that she has the capacity to be a major brat and that she is, in many respects, an unexceptional young girl who loves movies and sweets and is the ultimate desiring and gullible consumer.
- Humbert tries to keep her away from other kids, especially boys. Lolita does a lot of pouting.
- Humbert examines the ethics of his behavior, making all sorts of twists in logic to justify what he does. He also threatens Lolita that if she tells on him she will end up in a juvenile detention home.
- They continue to push westward. Humbert details the landscape and natural beauty. They traveled from August 1947 to August 1948, avoiding Florida and Lolita's birthplace. They

end up in the northeastern college town of Beardsley.

Book 2, Chapter 2

- Humbert reflects upon the range of experiences he and Lolita had during their travels around the United States – all of which were, he admits, to keep her in good humor so he could have his way with her. They saw a lot of lowbrow tourist sights and ate a lot of bad food.
- Along the way they had their fights, and Humbert always felt an almost paranoid level of protectiveness about Lolita. She wants to pick up hitchhikers, but Humbert doesn't like the contact with other people or air of sexuality she puts off to men. He is keenly aware of her other interests.
- Lolita enjoys playing tennis and swimming. Humbert is happy to watch her in a swimming pool along with other frolicking adolescents.
- In California she begins taking tennis lessons. One day, Humbert notices a man talking to Lolita – he begins to get worried.
- Humbert enjoys playing games and manipulating Lolita to get sex out of her. He also likes reflecting on the important roles he plays in her life: "And I was such a thoughtful friend, such a passionate father, such a good pediatrician, attending to all the wants of my little auburn brunette's body!" (2.2.17). He is, here, referring to getting her a cup of coffee.

Book 2, Chapter 3

- Humbert cannot help but notice that Lolita is moving from indifference toward him to repulsion. That hurts.
- He admits that he is always trying to liberate himself from memories of his first nymphet, Miss. Leigh. He is haunted by their adolescent caresses on the beach.
- He enjoys having sex with Lolita in beautiful outdoor surroundings – though such places can be dangerous, as he finds out one day when a woman picking flowers sees them in post-coital embrace.
- Over the course of the year, they attend about 150 movies. Lolita loves the melodramatic, silly meaningless ones and Humbert enjoys sitting in the dark groping her. Again, he almost gets caught.
- Humbert digresses into thoughts of the legal aspects of his relationship to Lolita. Is he a legal guardian? Should he pursue this role? Does he want the attention from the courts? He could ask his old friend and neighbor Mr. Farlow, but he is too busy taking care of his wife, Jean, who now has cancer.
- Feeling pangs that he is not providing an education for Lolita, they settle in Beardsley where she will go to a school for girls and he can teach at the local women's college. He

can also hang out with an old friend named Gaston Godin.

- Humbert's income is getting low, so there's the money issue too. They return after a year of travel. As he cynically puts it, "We had been everywhere. We had really seen nothing" (2.3.19).
- Lolita sobs in bed every night. Unable to deal, Humbert pretends that he is sleeping.

Book 2, Chapter 4

- Gaston Godin helps Humbert find a house at Beardsley and they settle in at 14 Thayer Street, a house that bears a pathetic but uncanny resemblance to the old Haze house.
- At the Beardsley school, "an expensive day school" (2.4.3), Humbert meets Mrs. Pratt, who can't seem to get his name right and misinterprets Lolita and everything else. She lays out the school's educational philosophy, which is a bunch of nonsense.
- Beardsley is more of a finishing school than anything else; social skills are way more important than intellectual rigor and the focus is on the "four D's: Dramatics, Dance, Debating and Dating" (2.4.5).
- Humbert is consoled by the view from his Thayer Street house, which looks out on the school playground, where he hopes to watch Lolita and other nymphets through a set of powerful binoculars. Unfortunately, construction workers block the view soon after they move in.

Book 2, Chapter 5

- Humbert describes his various neighbors on Thayer Street and assesses the risk each one presents to his cozy little set-up with Lolita. Some of them are nosy about Lolita's mother so Humbert knows he has to be watchful.
- He voices particular concern about their cook, Mrs. Holigan, who thankfully is a little out of it. He wants to make sure that Lolita doesn't befriend her too much.

Book 2, Chapter 6

- Humbert describes Gaston Godin, a well-respected though truly unimpressive French professor who seems thoroughly uninterested in Humbert's relationship to Lolita. Based upon Humbert's description, Gaston seems to have his own bizarre tastes (which run toward young boys), so the two just enjoy each other's company and keep their private lives, well, private.

- They often play chess together in the Humbert home.
- Humbert reveals that Gaston later became embroiled in a nasty business in Naples, Italy.
- Despite his mediocrity and lack of inspiration, Gaston is a decent companion and something of a distraction and alibi.

Book 2, Chapter 7

- Humbert and Lolita are both sinking lower. Her morals, he explains, are dropping; he, on the other hand is weak.
- The small allowance he has allowed her has created a monster. Her demands for money in exchange for sex are becoming oppressive to Humbert. Concerned that Lolita is accumulating running money, Humbert periodically breaks into her room to steal back her money. She catches on to him and begins hiding the money elsewhere.

Book 2, Chapter 8

- Lolita's attraction to local boys has become a point of concern. For support, Humbert turns to a local advice column, which advises welcoming young male admirers to the house and making friends with them. Instead, Humbert creates a list of house rules that dictates her interactions with boys, such as where she can go, whom she can go with, and what she can do and discuss at such places. Lolita is, of course, angered by his hypocritical protectiveness.
- Humbert knows he can't stop her from doing everything and noses around her room to find evidence. He also watches her hawk-like when she talks to boys on the street. He experiences a deepening sense of jealousy and fear.
- At the same time, he congratulates himself for making all sorts of dazzling impressions on people, none of which include pervert or pedophile.

Book 2, Chapter 9

- Unfortunately for Humbert, Lolita's friends are really not nymphets. Her best friend, Mona Dahl, is a little too experienced for Humbert's liking.
- She also doesn't betray any secrets about Lolita, so is not useful to Humbert as a source of insider information. After interrogating her, Humbert can only detect that she has a crush on him. He worries that Lolita is setting him up.

Book 2, Chapter 10

- Even as Lolita tries to do her homework, Humbert cannot manage to stop mauling her and begging for sex. She is clearly fed up with his sexual appetites and begs to be left alone.

Book 2, Chapter 11

- Headmistress Pratt invites Humbert over for a little chat. Lolita's grades are poor and Pratt is concerned about the young girl's "onset of sexual maturing" (2.11.6).
- Pratt proceeds to offer a Freudian interpretation of Lolita's sexuality and a lengthy review of each teacher's thoughts on the pupil, Dolly Haze. Pratt recommends that Lolita be allowed to date boys and participate in the school play, *The Enchanted Hunters*.
- Humbert promises to talk all of the issues out with Lolita, then secretly considers marrying her so he can murder her.
- Humbert seeks out Lolita and offers her 65 cents for a sexual favor.

Book 2, Chapter 12

- Around Christmas, Lolita becomes very sick. When she recovers, Humbert consents to a "Party with Boys" (2.12.1) at the house.
- The party pretty much sucks and Lolita finds the boys "revolting" (2.12.3), a point of great relief to Humbert.
- For Lolita's birthday Humbert buys her a bicycle and a book about American painting.

Book 2, Chapter 13

- Lolita becomes obsessed with *The Enchanted Hunters*, the play she is working on at school in which she plays the farmer's daughter.
- Humbert can't be bothered to read the play, because he is too busy working. He does note the coincidence of the play's name and the name of the first hotel in which he and Lolita had sex. He doesn't bring that point up to Lolita because he is sure she will be indifferent.
- He reflects upon his thoughts of the play, which were that it was part of some local tradition, a silly little schoolchild's fantasy story rather than the reality that it was some

work by a noted playwright and had recently been produced in New York.
- Surprisingly, Lolita brings up the title of the play one day, asking Humbert if it was the hotel where he raped her.

Book 2, Chapter 14

- Lolita is also taking piano lessons with Miss Emperor. Unfortunately, she has not been attending them – which Humbert only discovers when the teacher calls after several weeks' absence. Humbert saves face by remaining calm. When confronted, Lolita lies by saying that she has been rehearsing the play in the park with Mona. Mona covers for her, much to Humbert's irritation.
- When Humbert returns to discuss the lie with Lolita, he cannot help but notice how much she has changed over the past two years. She has, since their affair began, developed poor skin and a general physical filth that is not at all nymphet-like. Her body is more muscular and mature and her make-up looks tawdry.
- Humbert threatens to pull Lolita out of Beardsley if she continues lying. The fight turns physical and ugly, with Lolita accusing Humbert of committing all manner of sordid and murderous acts, some of which are true.
- When a neighbor calls to complain about the shouting, Lolita slips out of the house. A frantic Humbert flies down the street and finds Lolita in a telephone booth talking on the phone.
- Lolita confesses that she hates Beardsley and wants to leave – but *she* gets to decide where they go. When he agrees, they reconcile by going home to have sex because Lolita feels "romantic" (2.14.32).

Book 2, Chapter 15

- Humbert readies the car for the trip and tells Lolita's school that he has been hired as a chief consultant to a Hollywood movie about existentialism.
- Lolita has traced the exact route they will take and Humbert is touched that she is taking such care in the trip. He appreciates her curiosity.
- As they are leaving town a familiar looking woman (Edusa Gold) pulls up along side their car and expresses disappointment that Lolita has pulled out of the school play. When asked, Lolita says that the play was written by "Some old woman, Clare Something" (2.15.6).
- Humbert says he thinks it's odd that she was so passionate about the play only to lose interest so abruptly.

Book 2, Chapter 16

- Back to a series of second-rate motels, now a little more developed and hotel-like.
- Humbert begins reflecting on what he calls "McFate," thinking about all of the elements that converged to bring him where he is.
- He begins suspecting that Lolita is communicating with someone as she often disappears for short periods, excusing herself to use the toilet.
- Lolita has become moodier, often changing her mind about their destination and wanting to lie about and read magazines all day.
- One day, returning from the market, Humbert gets a strange feeling as he approaches their cabin. Lolita, who refused to get out bed before, is now completely dressed. She was up to something while he was out. She has a strange glow.

Book 2, Chapter 17

- Humbert mentions that he has a gun that previously belonged to the late Harold Haze (Lolita's father). Farlow taught him to use it in the forest near Hourglass Lake.

Book 2, Chapter 18

- Humbert and Lolita are definitely being followed as they continue their journey west. Humbert refers to his shadow as "Detective Trapp," identifiable by the "Aztec Red Convertible" he drives (2.18.1).
- Not knowing that "another Humbert was avidly following Humbert and Humbert's nymphet" (2.18.2), he actually thinks they are being pursued by a detective. Still, he considers that he may be just going mad and hallucinating all of the evidence that they are being watched.
- One day, he actually does witness Lolita talking to a man with whom she seems quite familiar. He bears a strong resemblance to Humbert's relative Gustave Trapp, which is where the nickname Detective Trapp comes from. Lolita says she was just giving him directions, but Humbert doesn't buy it.
- They arrive in the town of Wace where they attend a summer theatre production. The images of the play distinctly recall the work of James Joyce, and he considers that the authors, Clare Quilty and Vivian Darkbloom, lifted the idea directly from Joyce. A passing view of the authors excites Lolita, which Humbert finds peculiar.
- Teasingly, Humbert says "I thought [...] Quilty was an ancient flame of yours, in the days when you loved me, in sweet old Ramsdale" (2.18.32).

Book 2, Chapter 19

- They stop in a post office in Wace. Humbert intercepts a letter from Mona, which he promptly reads. When he looks up from the letter, Lolita is nowhere to be seen.
- After much panic, he finds her. She says she ran into a friend from Beardsley. Again, Humbert knows she is lying.
- Humbert is angered by Lolita's slippery ways and announces that he has recorded the license plate of the car that is following them. He opens the glove compartment to produce the evidence only to find she has erased some of the numbers. He slaps her across the face. He knows they are doomed.
- Now Humbert believes he is seeing Trapp in other cars. One day when he gets a flat tire, he decides to confront Trapp, who quickly speeds off. Humbert is fairly sure he is losing his mind and becoming homicidal.

Book 2, Chapter 20

- Humbert believes that Lolita's dramatic training has taught her how to betray him. Nonetheless, he enjoys playing audience to her performances. She is such a vision in her tennis get-up that Humbert would like to film her. She has become quite the graceful and athletic tennis player. She doesn't really enjoy the game and prefers swimming and acting. Humbert admits that he just loves games, chess included because they all have a certain "magic" (2.20.13).
- In Colorado, Lolita begins playing quite a bit of tennis. On one particular day, Humbert goes to fetch some refreshments. A man informs him that he has received an important call from the head of Beardsley school. He suspects that the call was an elaborate distraction and checks on Lolita.
- Lolita is still playing tennis, now with some odd character whose familiarity with her unnerves Humbert. When he asks her doubles partners about the man, they play dumb.

Book 2, Chapter 21

- By the pool later, Humbert sees a creepy man watching Lolita. His look is recognizable to Humbert. What really irks Humbert is that Lolita *knows* the man is watching her and is obviously performing to his gaze.
- Humbert realizes that he is none other than the suspicious Trapp. All Humbert can do is drink gin.

Book 2, Chapter 22

- Humbert considers that the suspicions about Trapp are part of his "persecution mania" (2.22.1), a product of his addled brain.
- Lolita comes down with a terrible fever. He cannot avoid taking her to the hospital and finds that he must, to his great disappointment and fear, leave her on the hands of the doctors. Humbert is now convinced that her illness is part of a plan involving her "secret lover" (2.22.3).
- Humbert visits her many times, bringing her books and flowers. One day he notices a crumpled envelope on her tray and gets strange vibes from the nurse who claims it belongs to her.
- Now Humbert feels sick, but insists that he will pick up Lolita from the hospital the next day. When he phones the hospital, they inform him that her uncle, Mr. Gustave, has retrieved her and that they will meet Humbert at "Grandpa's ranch as agreed" (2.22.28).
- Humbert becomes crazed and barely manages to leave the hospital. He is glad he has a gun and vows to destroy his "brother" (2.22.29).

Book 2, Chapter 23

- Humbert begins to retrace the trip he took with Lolita, scouring hotel registries for clues to the driver of the red car.
- He visits all 342 hotels, and begins to gather clues about the abductor: clearly the man is messing with Humbert, as he leaves all sorts of suggestive names that indicate he is smug, clever, and knows French. Like Humbert, the man "was versed in logodaedaly and logomancy" (2.23.5), which means he has a big vocabulary. He also enjoys provoking Humbert with suggestive and allusive names.
- Humbert realizes he had been on their tail a long time.

Book 2, Chapter 24

- Humbert returns to Beardsley and continues his mad search for Lolita. All of his leads turn out to be dead ends.
- A private detective Humbert hires cannot even find her.

Book 2, Chapter 25

- Humbert announces: "This book is about Lolita" (2.25.1), proceeding to explain that the story will now be about the loss of her. She haunts him. He finally ships all of her clothes off to an orphanage near Canada.
- Humbert returns to the sanitarium, where he composes a missing persons ad in verse. He describes the poem as a "maniac's masterpiece" (2.25.20).
- Soon he meets Rita.

Book 2, Chapter 26

- Rita is *not* a nymphet – she is in her twenties and has a shady history. They become companions. Together they travel to California, as he continues looking for Lolita and doing some heavy drinking. He takes her to some of the hotels he and Lolita stayed at, in a desperate attempt to relive those moments. He has, in a sense, given up on finding her.
- He returns to the town in which The Enchanted Hunters hotel is located. He goes to the library for a little research trip. In the town's paper, *Briceland Gazette*, dated mid-August 1947, he seeks the photograph that was taken of him in the hotel lobby two years before.
- Rita is drinking heavily and becoming fearful that Humbert will leave her.

Book 2, Chapter 27

- Humbert receives a letter from Lolita, an event that makes him dizzy. The date is September, 1952.
- He also receives a letter from John Farlow. John writes that Jean has died and his life has undergone many changes. He needs information about Lolita because someone wants to buy the old Haze house.
- From Lolita's letter (which notably begins, "Dear Dad"), Humbert finds out that she is married and pregnant. Her husband, Dick, is on the brink of a big job in Alaska and she needs money. She also says that she has "gone through much sadness and hardship" (2.27.6). She is afraid Humbert is mad at her and so doesn't give her home address. The letter is signed "Dolly (Mrs. Richard F. Schiller)."

Book 2, Chapter 28

- Humbert leaves a sleeping Rita and sets off to find Lolita. Locating her town, he is

prepared for a duel to the death with her husband, whom he assumes is the man who stole her from him.

- Preparing to see her, he cleans and dresses himself. It takes a little tracking down to find her house as she has moved. He finally locates her house, on "Hunter Road" (2.28.5). It's a grim little shanty. He double-checks that he has his gun.

Book 2, Chapter 29

- Lolita, large and pregnant and wearing glasses, answers the door. Lolita indicates that her husband is working on a nearby shack. She explains that Dick knows nothing of her sordid past with Humbert. She is still beautiful, though a far cry from the nymphet he once knew.
- Humbert interrogates her about the man who stole her from him. Needing money, Lolita confesses, the mystery man was "the only man she had ever been crazy about" (2.29.30). The man had an uncle in Ramsdale and had spotted her with Humbert at The Enchanted Hunters hotel; his name is Clare Quilty.
- Lolita introduces her ordinary blue-collar husband to her "father." Humbert can hardly dislike the guy; in fact he sort of pities his simplicity.
- Humbert continues to question Lolita. He wants to know what happened to her lover. He accuses her of betraying him. She confesses that she was warned about "Cue" (the lover) because he liked little girls and had almost been jailed once for this criminal preference.
- After Quilty snatched Lolita from the hospital, they wound up at a ranch where Cue and his friends took part in all manner of orgy-like practices (including making porn films) that Lolita wanted nothing to do with. Cue kicked her out. Lolita got a job as a waitress and met Dick.
- Though worn and exhausted looking, Lolita still appeals to Humbert. He will always love her; he begs her to leave with him, promising that they will "live happily ever after" (2.29.68). She offers sex for the money she needs, but he explains that he wants her, not the sex.
- He gives her four thousand dollars. Lolita says she would never return to him. She would sooner go back to Cue. Extremely choked up, Humbert leaves.

Book 2, Chapter 30

- Humbert is now determined to find Ivor Quilty, which will be his way of finding the nephew, Cue.
- In an attempt to take a shortcut through the woods, Humbert gets stuck in a rainstorm, his car lodged in mud. He is in an emotional fog of rage and nostalgia.

Book 2, Chapter 31

- On the way to Ramsdale from Coalmont, Humbert reflects on his "case" (2.31.1), particularly with respect to a priest he once knew in Quebec. The two used to discuss the existence of God and other religious questions.
- He begins to experience deep guilt over the immorality of his relationship to Lolita and how he perpetrated his "foul lust" (2.31.1) on her. As he sees it, Humbert robbed Lolita of her childhood with his depravity.

Book 2, Chapter 32

- In retrospect, Humbert recognizes that he never knew Lolita as a person; to him, she was only a sex object. He recalls a poignant remark she once made about death.
- Humbert begins to address Lolita directly, confessing that, though he was a vile monster, he truly loved her.
- He recalls a moment in Beardsley when Lolita cried at the sight of her friend having a normal interaction with her own father. He also describes a time when Lolita confronted him about her mother, whom she refers to as "my murdered mummy" (2.32.6). As awful as Charlotte was, she still offered Lolita a far better life than he ever did.

Book 2, Chapter 33

- Humbert returns to the Haze home in Ramsdale. A nymphet is playing on the lawn. His filthy clothes scare the girl so he quickly retreats.
- Humbert feigns the need for some dental work so he can get an appointment with Ivor Quilty. During his dental exam, he questions Ivor about his nephew's whereabouts. The dentist admits he has not seen him in a long time, but that he must be at his ancestral home on Grimm Road.
- Humbert hastily departs, insulting the dentist and imagining shooting the gun.

Book 2, Chapter 34

- Humbert stakes out Pavor manor, Clare Quilty's home on Grimm Road. He imagines all sorts of unsavory characters there. He decides to return in the morning.
- Finding one of Lolita's old bobby pins in the glove compartment, Humbert has a twinge of nostalgia.

- He passes a drive-in on the way back to his motel room. On the large screen, he sees a man raising a gun.

Book 2, Chapter 35

- The next morning, Humbert double checks his gun (which he calls Chum) and returns to Pavor Manor. He enters the house only to find dead silence. He explores the house, which is huge and meandering with curious details throughout.
- Quilty finally emerges from one of the bathrooms and greets Humbert with complete indifference. Humbert marvels at finally having his nemesis trapped. Quilty responds with a complete blank at the mention of Lolita's name. Quilty's smugness irritates Humbert, who proceeds to inform Quilty that he is Lolita's father and that Quilty is about to die.
- Finally acknowledging who Lolita was, Quilty defends that he "saved her from a beastly pervert" (2.35.44). Quilty makes every effort to distract Humbert with clever witticisms and half-hearted excuses. They begin to wrestle over the gun.
- Humbert reads a list of Quilty's crimes written as a poem.
- Quilty tries bribing Humbert with the house, royalties from his play, pornography, young girls…but Humbert shoots at him.
- A chase ensues in which Quilty runs throughout the house trying to escape. Humbert shoots him several times. He turns out to be hard to kill, but Humbert eventually gets him.
- Humbert finds a group of drunk partiers downstairs and announces to them that he has just killed Quilty. They don't seem to care.

Book 2, Chapter 36

- Driving away, Humbert notices that he is covered with Quilty's blood. Having committed murder, he decides to drive on the wrong side of the street. He gets out of the car and waits to get arrested.
- He reflects on the sounds of children playing and feels profound guilt that he deprived Lolita of the simple pleasures of youthful innocence.
- That is his story. It took him 56 days to write *Lolita*, which he started in the psychiatric ward.
- He is opposed to capital punishment but thinks he should get 35 years in jail for rape.
- He ends the book by addressing Lolita, hoping that she lives a decent life, treats her husband and child well and does not mourn the death of Quilty. The book he has written is their way to share immortality.

Themes

Theme of Language and Communication

In *Lolita*, words are Humbert's greatest weapon and favorite toy. He is verbally adept and constantly assessing others based upon their ability to use language. Because he talks about words so much *and* happens to be our narrator, we have to watch out for him. Since he has been instructed to tell his story by his lawyer, we can be sure that he will take every opportunity to cast a favorable light on his behavior.

While Humbert certainly fesses up to unforgivable bad behavior, he still offers highly poetic descriptions that serve to distract the reader from the subject at hand. If it weren't for his skill with language, we would be faced with a stark account of Humbert's crime; instead, he makes the story an appealing one in spite of the grisly subject matter. In other words, he makes a story of rape, pedophilia, incest, murder, and exploitation beautiful and "enchants" the reader into sympathizing with him. He is particularly drawn to language of magic and fascination, fairy-tale like images, and references to "magic potion" (1.27.138), "crystal sleep" (1.28.1), and other dreamy images. He also makes appeals through legal language, sneaking in justifications and defenses of his behavior. To understand the full extent of his love of words and his manipulation of the reader, keep your *Oxford English Dictionary* at arm's reach!

Questions About Language and Communication

1. How does Humbert use language to manipulate our reception of his story?
2. Why does Humbert deny that he is a poet?
3. What does Humbert have in common with Clare Quilty – aside from a shared obsession with Lolita?
4. Humbert loves playing with words and, in particular, names. Why would he choose such a silly alias for himself?

Chew on Language and Communication

Language is Humbert's best friend (all he has to "play with") and his worst enemy, because he cannot help but detail his obsession with Lolita.

Love of words ties Humbert to Quilty more closely than Humbert would like to admit.

Theme of Love

Humbert spends a lot of time talking about love, particularly when describing his feelings for Lolita. Is it even possible that he loves her? The fact that he is our narrator and controls all of the images we see makes it difficult to know if he is using love as some sort of perverse excuse

for his behavior. Understanding his feelings is also complicated by the fact that he is writing the book in retrospect – reflecting and recording his story many years after the events have occurred. Part of our challenge as the reader is to try to understand the nature of his "love" for Lolita and try not to be wooed by him ourselves. Humbert prides himself on his skill in seduction and his efforts definitely extend to the reader as well. In his essay, "The Last Lover: Vladimir Nabokov's *Lolita*," Lionel Trilling once insisted, "Lolita is about love. Perhaps I shall be better understood if I put the statement in this form: Lolita is not about sex, but about love." Is there any way to see this novel as an American love story?

Questions About Love

1. Are any characters loyal? Does *Lolita* have any actual romance in it?
2. Is it possible that Humbert actually loves Lolita?
3. What is the purpose of Humbert's relationship with Rita?

Chew on Love

Humbert uses the idea of love to appeal to the romantic interests of his reader, believing that it will make his actions seem less disturbing.

Lolita's love of Quilty is one of the more inexplicable relationships of the novel.

Theme of Sex

From the outset, Humbert describes Lolita as "fire of my loins" (1.1.1). To be fair, he also calls her "light of my life" (1.1.1). But the question is: which is it? Is it possible for her to be both? The book has often been referred to as porn, but the author of the Foreword insists that the sex must be kept in for moral purposes, noting that "not a single obscene term is to be found in the whole work" (Fore.4). Truth be told, there is a lot of lust in *Lolita* – Humbert's and Clare Quilty's, mostly. And Lolita participates in her fair share of voluntary sexual activity – at Camp Q, especially. Much of the sex in the novel is very dark and perverse, criminal even, with rape, pedophilia, and incest at the front of the line.

Questions About Sex

1. Is any sex in the novel normal, not transgressive?
2. Why does Nabokov make Lolita so sexual and sexually experienced?
3. Is Humbert actually a "sex maniac," as he denies?

Chew on Sex

Humbert plays up Lolita's sexual experience in order to make his exploitation of her seem less outrageous.

Sexual attraction is the only way Humbert can relate to women.

Theme of Youth

Humbert is sexually obsessed with youth in *Lolita*. He doesn't care that he is aging; in fact he never mentions that. He is obsessed with "nymphets," young girls aged nine to fourteen. He does not hesitate to mention that once girls get past that age they are no longer attractive to him. College-age girls are way out of his age-range. Sure, Humbert recognizes all of the unrefined silliness and consumer vulgarity of youth, but that's a small price to pay. Sitting on a park bench watching young girls play hopscotch and skip rope, Humbert is in bliss: "Let them play around me forever. Never grow up" (1.5.11).

Questions About Youth

1. What does Humbert love about youth? What does he despise about it?
2. How does Humbert's own youth determine the rest of his life?
3. Does Humbert rob Lolita of her youth, as he suggests?

Chew on Youth

Humbert reads youth almost exclusively through a sexual lens, struggling to see that innocence as anything other than a quality to exploit.

Humbert's disgust of youth sits in a strange relation to his love of it.

Theme of Innocence

There is very little true innocence in *Lolita* and the sad part is that Humbert's attraction to innocence always means that he wants to take advantage of it. The idea of innocence in the novel refers first to Humbert's lack of it. He is, after all, telling his story from jail, where he sits rotting because he murdered someone. Though he recounts the story of his affair with Lolita, he doesn't try to play off that he didn't do anything wrong, but he does try to win the reader to his side. In other words, he's not innocent (far from it), but there are all sorts of reasons for what he did and they often involve a lack of innocence on the part of others.

Innocence also emerges as a theme in connection to America, a country that has fully embraced consumer possibilities, shallow movie magazines, and popular culture. Humbert links Lolita's lack of innocence to all of this American-ness, but he also makes a point of explaining that Lolita was not a virgin when he got to her and that she seduced him. In other words, he did

—

not steal her innocence.

Questions About Innocence

1. Does Humbert have any respect for innocence?
2. What are we supposed to think about all of Lolita's sexual experiences at age twelve? Are they supposed to change they way we feel about Humbert's crime?
3. What are the moral implications of Humbert murdering Quilty?

Chew on Innocence

Humbert is not only guilty of Quilty's death, but of Charlotte's as well.

Humbert's perversions mean that he actually finds childhood innocence sexy.

Theme of Justice and Judgment

It's easy to forget that the entire memoir is supposed to present a realistic and historical account of the relationship between Humbert and Lolita and how it led to the murder of Clare Quilty. Throughout *Lolita*, Humbert, our criminal narrator, refers to the readers as his jury, making appeals and presenting "evidence" to gain sympathy. He does make gestures toward admitting that he is a monster and a maniac who deprived Lolita of her youth, but he also dares the reader (and the jury) to prove it. In other words, he never takes full blame. From the beginning we know he is imprisoned for committing a crime, but the exact nature of it remains unknown. Did he murder Charlotte or Lolita? We do know that as he writes his story, he is waiting to be judged and so takes every opportunity to slip in a defense. However, he dies before his trial begins.

Questions About Justice and Judgment

1. There is a lot of death at a young age in the novel. Do these deaths imply any sense of judgment about the characters?
2. What purpose does the oddly stiff introduction by John Ray Jr., Ph.D. serve? Does it actually establish a way of reading the novel or is it soon forgotten?
3. How does Quilty's crime differ from Humbert's, if at all?

Chew on Justice and Judgment

By dying before his trial, Humbert never faces justice. It is unlikely that his memoir would have presented convincing defense material.

While Humbert's crime against Quilty is one of passion, his crime against Lolita is far more calculated.

Theme of Morality and Ethics

Despite his many efforts at defense in *Lolita*, Humbert knows he has committed some serious violations – referring to himself as a monster, a spider, a maniac, and a hound – but it is unclear whether these self-incriminations are just gestures for the reader (and jury). Humbert certainly references the ethical dilemma he is in, but it is never so great as to prevent him from perpetrating on Lolita.

He does admit that through the memoir he intends to prove that he is not a scoundrel, but he cannot resist the descriptions of his lust. He is torn between ethics and ego, law and lust. He offers many defenses for what he has done – psychological (trying to recover from losing Annabel), legal and literary (it may be illegal here and now, but look at East India, and what about Dante and Beatrice, Petrarch and Laureen?), and personal (after all Lolita was experienced and seduced *me*). The degree of his justification is proven here: just because he wasn't the first to get to Lolita and just because she seduced him, he says it's OK that he carries on for years as he does. Plus his whole nymphet, enchantment, demoniac theme intends to imply that he just couldn't help himself!

Questions About Morality and Ethics

1. What is the moral of the story? Is there one? Can we pin down Nabokov's message?
2. What kind of punishment does Humbert deserve? Does he redeem himself at all by writing the book?
3. Does Lolita bear *any* responsibility for her extended victimization?

Chew on Morality and Ethics

Humbert pays some lip-service to ethical questions, but usually goes right back to justifying his actions.

While Lolita seems able to move past what she has experienced, Humbert remains unreconciled even at the end, because he really does not acknowledge the extent of his violations.

Theme of Visions of America

Clearly Humbert has been obsessed with America from an early age, exposed as he was to idealized images of its grand panoramas and natural wonders. His trips across America in *Lolita* detail this fascination (and repulsion). He scrutinizes every absurd tourist trap, crappy motel, consumer habit, national compulsion, and stereotype of American culture. He both rejects the

fussy, musty ways of Europe and plays upon American perceptions of the sophisticated European intellectual. To him, Charlotte represents the worst of American culture: an unthinking, mediocre, upstart with pretentions to cultural sophistication. Still, he is all too ready to let her fantasize about his European background.

Though Humbert recognizes all of Lolita's bad-mannered, outspoken, brash American-ness, he gives her a pass, and in fact embraces her slang and love of lowbrow magazines and Hollywood movies. Unlike her mother, she utterly repudiates, even mocks, his pretense to cleverness and refuses to be reformed or refined by him. Humbert often covertly associates Lolita with America, praising their shared youth and vulgarity. His admission that he has defiled America bears a strong parallel to his treatment of Lolita. Nabokov himself was hurt by accusations that the book was "un-American," an assessment, in his words, that "pains me considerably more than the idiotic accusation of immorality" (source: James Kincaid, "Lolita at Middle Age"). America is the land of mass culture, a modern society of consumer goods, a nation of tourist sights and souvenirs, where everything is commodified and collectable.

Questions About Visions of America

1. What role does America play as a setting for the novel?
2. What does Humbert like and dislike about America?
3. In what ways does Humbert associate Lolita with America?
4. What does Humbert dislike about the "Old World" (Europe)?

Chew on Visions of America

Even as Humbert mocks American consumerism as a cultural habit, he engages in a sinister form of it by using up Lolita's childhood.

The American setting is absolutely crucial to the novel's themes of youth and consumerism.

Language and Communication Quotes

Lo-lee-ta: the tip of the tongue taking a trip of three steps down the palate to tap, at three, on the teeth. Lo. Lee. Ta. (1.1.1)

Thought: Everything about Lolita fills Humbert with pleasure, even the feeling of saying her name. There is no single part of her that he does not turn into a fetish object.

You can always count on a murderer for a fancy prose style. (1.1.3)

Thought: Humbert loves to make striking statements. Not only does he confess a crime early in the novel, but he also draws attention to the quality of his own writing.

Let me remind you my reader that in England [...] the term "girl-child" is defined as "a girl who is over eight but under fourteen. (1.5.9)

Thought: Humbert pays close attention to definitions. He is also eager to sway his readers, whom he often addresses as his "jury."

Quine the Swine. Guilty of killing Quilty. Oh, my Lolita, I have only words to play with! (1.8.4)

Thought: Beware of anyone who has this much fun with words. Could be actually be telling us how to read his own book?

Humbert Humbert is also infinitely moved by the little one's slangy speech. (1.11.5)

Thought: Humbert is charmed by Lolita's misuse of the language. Part of her charm is her typical American adolescent way of talking.

But I am no poet. I am only a very conscientious recorder. (1.17.7)

Thought: Do we believe either of Humbert's claims? Watch for contradictions to this claim of straightforward reporting.

Let us, however, forget, Dolores Haze, so-called legal terminology, terminology that accepts as rational the term "lewd and lascivious cohabitation." I am not a criminal sexual psychopath taking indecent liberties with a child [. . .] I am your daddum. (2.1. 11)

Thought: Humbert spends a lot of time rationalizing his behavior. Somehow, if he can convince Lolita and the reader, perhaps he can also convince himself.

At the very first motel office I visited, Ponderosa Lodge, his entry, among a dozen obviously human ones, read: Dr. Gratiano Forbeson, Mirandola, NY. Its Italian Comedy connotations could not fail to strike me, of course. (2.23.4)

Thought: Humbert had found in Clare Quilty a worthy rival. They are both lovers of language and of Lolita.

His allusions were definitely highbrow. He was well-read. He knew French. He was versed in logodaedaly and logomancy. (2.23.5)

Thought: Humbert cannot help but respect Lolita's abductor because of his deft language skills. Because Quilty is like him, Humbert both admires and despises him.

"Quilty," I said, "do you recall a little girl called Dolores Haze, Dolly Haze? Dolly called Dolores, Colo.?" (2.35.2)

Thought: Even in the culmination moment of confrontation with Quilty, Humbert engages in word play with Lolita's name.

Love Quotes

All at once we were madly, clumsily, shamelessly, agonizingly in love with each other; hopelessly, I should add, because the frenzy of mutual possession might have been assuaged only by our actually imbibing and assimilating every particle of each other's soul and flesh. (1.3.3)

Thought: Humbert poetically describes his feelings for his first love, Annabel. His affection is almost like a desire to consume. This imagery will return with Lolita.

I broke her spell by incarnating her in another. (1.3.4)

Thought: Humbert often describes love in fairy tale terms. Lolita cures him of his thwarted love of his first nymphet.

I knew that I had fallen in love with Lolita forever; but I also knew she would not forever be Lolita. (1.15.3)

Thought: Humbert expresses genuine feelings of love toward Lolita, which are often difficult to process given his treatment of her. As suggested here, however, the love seems contingent on Lolita being a nymphet. Does this turn out to be true?

You see, there is no alternative. I have loved you from the minute I saw you. I am a passionate and lonely woman and you are the love of my life. (1.16.2)

Thought: Charlotte's impassioned letter to Humbert is received with disgust and delight. Though at first repulsed, Humbert manages to make her love of him part of his plan.

"But we are lovers, aren't we?" (1.27.43)

Thought: Lolita reveals herself as far more precocious savvy than we or Humbert even knew. She knows they are lovers before Humbert even makes his first (sort of) real move. Do we believe this?

and I looked and looked at her and knew clearly as I know I am to die, that I loved her more than anything I had ever seen or imagined on earth, or hoped for anywhere else. (2.29.67)

Thought: It is difficulty to reconcile Humbert's deep love of Lolita and his predatory ways. Do we believe him when he makes these claims? Does he love her or the idea of her?

He was the only man she had ever been crazy about [...] And I had never counted, of course? (2.29.30)

Thought: Learning that Lolita actually loved Clare Quilty is deeply disturbing. How can this be? Humbert longs to know her feelings for him, even after so many years.

"Lolita," I said, "this may be neither here nor there but I have to say it. Life is very short. From here to that old car you know so well there is a stretch of twenty, twenty-five paces. It is a very short walk. Make those twenty-five steps. Now. Right now. Come just as you are. And we shall live happily ever after." (2.29.68)

Thought: Humbert's last ditch effort to win Lolita back stirs feelings in the reader. Do we actually want her to leave Dick and return to Humbert? What's the deal?

I loved you. I was a pentapod monster, but I loved you. I was despicable and brutal, and turpid, and everything, mais je t'aimais, je t'aimais . (2.32:4)

Thought: Humbert writes a lot about loving Lolita. His expressions of love and expressions of guilt often go together. Why?

But while the blood still throbs through my writing hand, you are still as much part of blessed matter as I am, and I can still talk to you from here to Alaska […] And this is the only immortality you and I may share, my Lolita. (2.36.7)

Thought: Nothing can ever really divide him from Lolita. Writing the book assures that, in a certain way, they will be together forever.

Sex Quotes

was my excessive desire for that child only the first evidence of an inherent singularity? (1.4.1)

Thought: Humbert never stops trying to puzzle out the source of his perverse desires. These efforts are interesting in light of his deep dislike of psychoanalysis.

Her legs, her lovely live legs, were not too close together, and when my hand located what it sought, a dreamy and eerie expression, half-pleasure and half-pain, came over those childish features. (1.4.3)

Thought: Humbert details his first sexual experience. Of course there has to be some pain involved.

While a college student, in London and Paris, paid ladies sufficed me. (1.5.1)

Thought: If he can't have nymphets, Humbert will take prostitutes. Most of his sexual experiences involve some sort of vice.

[…] inly, I was consumed by a hell furnace of localized lust for every passing nymphet whom as a law-abiding poltroon I never dared approach. (1.5.8)

Thought: Humbert must focus to control his urges. The fact that young girls are hands off in the eyes of the law does actually mean something to him, sort of.

All of which goes to show how dreadfully stupid poor Humbert always was in matters of sex. (1.7.1)

Thought: Humbert loses no opportunity to tell us how smart he is. When it comes to sex, though, his judgment stinks.

With awe and delight [...] I saw again her lovely indrawn abdomen where my southbound mouth had briefly paused; and those puerile hips on which I had kissed the crenulated imprint left by the band of her shorts. (1.10.12)

Thought: Humbert's first glimpse of Lolita conjures visions of Annabel. That's it, he's moving in…

[...] focusing my lust and rocking slightly under my newspaper, I felt that my perception of her, if properly concentrated upon might be sufficient to have me attain a beggar's bliss immediately. (1.11.7)

Thought: Humbert finally figures out a way to gratify himself without Lolita knowing. Has he already crossed the line? Is Lolita already on to him?

Her kiss, to my delirious embarrassment, had some rather comical refinements of flutter and probe which made me conclude she had been coached by a Lesbian. (1.29.14)

Thought: Much to Humbert's surprise, he is not Lolita's first sexual experience. He is at once surprised, pleased, and disturbed by this realization.

"You mean [...] you mean you will give us that money only if I go with you to a motel. Is that what you mean?" (2.29.70)

Thought: A desperate Lolita can only see Humbert as an old pervert. She cannot grasp that his generosity does not have sexual strings attached.

"You see I had no fun with your Dolly. I am practically impotent, to tell the melancholy truth." (2.35.46)

Thought: Though he stole Lolita from Humbert, Clare Quilty did not have the same lust as Humbert – or so he says. So what did he want from her? Do we believe that he is impotent?

Youth Quotes

In point of fact, there might have been no Lolita at all had I not loved, one summer, an initial girl-child. (1.1.3)

Thought: Humbert often describes Lolita as his own creation, his figment of nymphet perfection. We need to be careful as readers, because all we know of Lolita comes from him.

The spiritual and the physical had been blended in us with a perfection that must remain incomprehensible to the matter-of-fact, crude, standard-brained youngsters of today. (1.4.2)

Thought: Humbert has very romantic ideas about his first love. He also doesn't think much of the manners of children. How do these two points work together?

Now I wish to introduce the following idea. Between the age limits of nine and fourteen there occur maidens who, to certain bewitched travelers, twice or many times older than they, reveal their true nature which is not human, but nymphic (that is, demoniac); and these chosen creatures I propose to designate as "nymphets." (1.5.5)

Thought: Humbert's definition of nymphet is very precise. He wants to make sure that the reader knows exactly the kind of girl he adores. Why is this information so important to him? Isn't it incriminating?

The bud-stage of breast development begins early (10.7 years) in the sequence of somatic changes accompanying pubescence. And the next maturational item available is the first appearance of pigmented pubic hair (11.2 years). (1.5.9)

Thought: Humbert has clearly spent a lot of time thinking about the bodies of adolescent girls. His scientific descriptions make him seem like an even bigger pervert.

Never grow up. (1.5.11)

Thought: Humbert has a lot of strange notions about children. He often expresses contradictory feelings of desire and disgust toward children.

A modern child, an avid reader of movie magazines, an expert in dream-like close-ups, might not think it too strange, I guessed, if a handsome, intensely virile grown-up friend [...] (1.11.22)

Thought: Humbert's self-perceptions are full of references to the movies. He often exploits the fact that others are so wrapped up in images from Hollywood. Does he love movies as much as Lolita does? How are movies a tool of his exploitation?

The whole point is that the old link between the adult world and the child world has been completely severed nowadays by new customs and new laws […] After all, Lolita was only twelve, and no matter what concessions I made to time and place—even bearing in mind the crude behavior of American schoolchildren—I still was under the impression that whatever went on among those brash brats, went on at a later age, and in a different environment. (1.28.2)

Thought: Humbert struggles with the obvious unattractive qualities in children. He often reluctantly confesses that Lolita is just as ordinary as the rest.

And so we rolled East, I more devastated than braced with the satisfaction of my passion, and she glowing with health; her bi-iliac garland still as brief as a lad's, although she had added two inches to her stature and eight pounds to her weight. (2.3.19)

Thought: OK, time to get out your dictionary. Humbert's obsession with certain parts of Lolita's young body is downright disturbing.

She was only the faint violet whiff and dead leaf of the nymphet I had rolled myself upon with such cries in the past (2.29.67)

Thought: At only seventeen, Lolita has lost the bloom of youth. Shades of the nymphet can barely be discerned when Humbert visits a pregnant and married Lolita. But he still loves her. What does that suggest?

Mid-twentieth century ideas concerning child-parent relationship have been considerably tainted by the scholastic rigmarole and standardized symbols of the psychoanalytic racket. (2.32.6)

Thought: Humbert is really down on psychoanalysis, but he also really likes invoking Freud's ideas. What's with his deep dislike of these ideas?

Innocence Quotes

Humbert tried hard to be good. Really and truly, he did. He had the utmost respect for ordinary children, with their purity and vulnerability, and under no circumstances would he have interfered with the innocence of a child, if there was the least risk of a row. (1.5.9)

Thought: This is a typical Humbert sentence. He loves to defend his ways, but ends up expressing something altogether different: he just doesn't want to get caught.

[…] it was she who seduced me. (1.29.12)

Thought: OK, this one's a real shocker. After all of his plans, Lolita is the one who makes the first move. Do we even believe him?!

This was a lone child, an absolute waif, with whom a heavy-limbed, foul-smelling adult had had strenuous intercourse three times that very morning. (1.32.25)

Thought: Sometimes Humbert manages to express some objectivity. Rather than seeing himself as a devilishly handsome movie actor, he sees himself for the beast he really is.

She groped for words. I supplied them mentally "He broke my heart. You merely broke my life." (2.29.81)

Thought: Humbert finds the truth from Lolita. His feelings of culpability are confirmed: he really did destroy Lolita's life.

[…] nothing could make my Lolita forget the foul lust I had inflicted upon her. Unless it can be proven to me—to me as I am now, today, with my heart and my beard, and my putrefaction—that in the infinite run it does not matter a jot that a North American girl-child named Dolores Haze had been deprived of her childhood by a maniac. (2.31.1)

Thought: Humbert considers the implications of what he has done. How does it affect her? How does it affect him? What does it mean in the larger scope of things? Is he even sincere?

And there were times when I knew how you felt, and it was hell to know it, my little one. Lolita girl, brave Dolly Schiller. (2.32.4)

Thought: Humbert does actually experience feelings of empathy. But his urges were always stronger than his compassion.

It had become gradually clear to my conventional Lolita during our singular and bestial cohabitation that even the most miserable of family lives was better than the parody of incest, which, in the long run, was the best I could offer the waif. (2.32.6)

Thought: Humbert acknowledges the depth of his depravity. Interesting that he sees it as the only option he had. Do we believe that he believes this nonsense?

All at once I noticed that from the lawn I had mown a golden-skinned, brown-haired nymphet of nine or ten, in white shorts, was looking at me with wild fascination in her large blue-black eyes. (2.33.3)

Thought: Returning one last time to the old Haze home, Humbert sees a nymphet. Has he changed at all?

"She was my child, Quilty." (2.35.25)

Thought: Humbert's long-awaited encounter with his nemesis. Should we be surprised that he plays the dad card? Why does he use this approach?

Reader! What I heard was but the melody of children at play, nothing but that, and so limpid was the air within this vapor of blended voices, majestic and minute, remote and magically near, frank and divinely enigmatic—one could hear now and then, as if released, an almost articulate spurt of vivid laughter [...] I stood listening to that musical vibration from my lofty slope [...] and then I knew that the hopelessly poignant thing was not Lolita's absence from my side, but the absence of her voice from that concord. (2.36.3)

Thought: Humbert makes a broad assessment of his crime. Humbert wants us to feel his pain. Should we?

Justice and Judgment Quotes

"Humbert Humbert," their author, had died in legal captivity, of coronary thrombosis, on November 16, 1952, a few days before his trial was scheduled to start. (Fore.1)

Thought: Such information does not have much meaning to us yet. We know already though that a certain criminal will not be brought to justice.

References to "H.H."'s crime may be looked up by the inquisitive in the daily papers for September-October 1952; its cause and purpose would have continued to remain a complete mystery, had not this memoir been permitted to come under my reading lamp. (Fore.2)

Thought: The author of the words is at pains to present the facts. He also wants us to know about the significance of what we are about to read. Consider these words as you proceed into the "memoir."

Ladies and gentlemen of the jury, exhibit number one. (1.1.4)

Thought: Humbert is addressing the reader. Does he think a jury will read his novel, or does he see the readers as his ultimate judges?

Ladies and gentlemen of the jury, the majority of sex offenders that hanker for some throbbing, sweet-moaning, physical but not necessarily coital, relation with a girl-child, are innocuous, inadequate, passive, timid strangers who merely ask the community to allow them to pursue their practically harmless, so-called aberrant behavior, their little hot wet private acts of sexual deprivation without the police and society cracking down on them. We are not sex fiends! (1.20.33)

Thought: Be careful when Humbert plays the lawyer. He is very convincing and sympathetic. How does he get to us?

"You're a monster. You're a detestable, abominable, criminal fraud. If you come near—I'll scream out the window. Get back!" (1.22.7)

Thought: Charlotte is one of the only people to express this disgust. Perhaps she is smarter than he gives her credit for.

"The word is incest," said Lo—and walked into the closet, walked out again with a young golden giggle [...] (1.27.108)

Thought: Lolita is way more attuned than Humbert thought she was. She often has moments of keen realization. Why doesn't she just run away?

"You chump [...] You revolting creature. I was a daisy-fresh girl, and look what you've done to me. I ought to call the police and tell them you raped me. Oh, you dirty, dirty old man." (1.32.33)

Thought: Lolita plays a lot of games with Humbert. She enjoys making these accusations and expressing disgust. Can we ever get a sense of what she is thinking?

"Because you took advantage of a sinner/because you took advantage/because you took/because you took advantage of my disadvantage [...] /because of all you did/because of all I did not/you have to die." (2.35.63, 73)

Thought: Humbert reads the allegations to Clare Quilty. How different is he from this enemy?

I stopped in the doorway and said: "I have just killed Clare Quilty." "Good for you," said the florid fellow as he offered one of the drinks to the elder girl. "Somebody ought to have done it long ago, remarked the fat man." (2.35.85)

Thought: There isn't much good behavior in this book. People often seem indifferent to death throughout the novel.

For reasons that may appear more obvious than they really are, I am opposed to capital punishment; this attitude will be, I trust, shared by the sentencing judge. Had I come before myself, I would have given Humbert at least thirty-five years for rape, and dismissed the rest of the charges. (2.36.6)

Thought: Not surprisingly, Humbert concludes his book by sentencing himself, in a way. Why does he think "the rest of the charges" should be dropped? What are "the rest of the charges"?

Morality and Ethics Quotes

If, however, for this paradoxical prude's comfort, an editor attempted to dilute or omit scenes that a certain type of mind might call "aphrodisiac" […], one would have to forego the publication of "Lolita" altogether, since those very scenes that one might ineptly accuse of a sensuous existence of their own, are the most strictly functional ones in the development of a tragic tale tending unswervingly to nothing less than a moral apotheosis. (Fore.4)

Thought: The person introducing *Lolita* to us has certain ideas he wants to express. He wants to prepare the reader for what we would call "adult content." Don't be aroused by the material or assume that it is there for gratuitous reasons: they had to include it for moral reasons.

No doubt ["H.H."] is horrible, he is abject, he is a shining example of moral leprosy, a mixture of ferocity and jocularity that betrays supreme misery perhaps, but is not conducive to attractiveness. (Fore.5)

Thought: The author in the introduction is really into the whole moral lesson of the novel. He also misreads Humbert in many ways. Reread this Foreword when you finish the novel.

When I try to analyze my own cravings, motives, actions and so forth, I surrender to a sport of retrospective imagination which feeds the analytic faculty with boundless alternatives and causes each visualized route to fork and re-fork without end in the maddeningly complex project of my past. (1.4.1)

Thought: OK, a lot of big words in here. Humbert really wants to turn the novel into an exercise of reflection, but it isn't easy.

One moment I was ashamed and frightened, another recklessly optimistic. Taboos strangled me. (1.5.9)

Thought: Even in his early days as a predator, Humbert is torn between desire and law. His emotions are all over the map.

I felt proud of myself. I had stolen the honey of a spasm without impairing the morals of a minor. Absolutely no harm done. (1.14.2)

Thought: Humbert comes up with ways to be an undetected pervert. He is not as covert as he thinks.

Simple, was it not? But what d'ye know, folks—I just could not make myself do it! (1.20.32)

Thought: Even wicked ol' Humbert couldn't kill Charlotte off to get at Lolita. But we already know he is a murderer…

Instead of basking in the beams of smiling Chance, I was obsessed with all sorts of purely ethical doubts and fears. (1.25.1)

Thought: In spite of the impression he makes of a self-indulgent pervert, Humbert does actually have a moral compass, so to speak. He makes it very challenging to establish a complete and clear portrait of his character.

A couple of years before, under the guidance of an intelligent French-speaking confessor, to whom, in a moment of metaphysical curiosity, I had turned over a Protestant's drab atheism for an old-fashioned popish cure, I had hoped to deduce from my sense of sin the existence of a Supreme Being. (2.31.1)

Thought: Humbert has considered his place in a world in which God exists. Whether he actually believes in God is not clear.

The moral sense in mortals is the duty / We have to pay on mortal sense of beauty. (2.31.2)

Thought: In a typical poetic flourish, Humbert tries to act as though it is his moral obligation to appreciate beauty. What does this little verse suggest about his willingness to be accountable for his behavior?

"We are men of the world, in everything—sex, free verse, marksmanship. If you bear me a grudge, I am ready to make unusual amends […] but really, my dear Mr. Humbert, you were not an ideal stepfather." (2.35.77)

Thought: Even though Quilty is a pervert, he does have a good point. Quilty is perhaps more honest about his flaws.

Visions of America Quotes

America, the country of rosy children and great trees, where life would be such an improvement on dull dingy Paris. (1.8.4)

Thought: Humbert draws many comparisons between Europe ("the Old World") and America. Consider all of the qualities he associates with America.

[Lolita] grasped [the apple] and bit into it, and my heart was like snow under thin crimson skin, and with the monkeyish nimbleness that was so typical of that American nymphet, she snatched out of my abstract grip the magazine. (1.13.6)

Thought: Humbert is aroused and amused by American children. Their freshness and friskiness is a source of endless fascination. How are they different from European children?

I know how reserved you are, how "British." Your old-world reticence, your sense of decorum may be shocked by the boldness of an American girl! (1.16.5)

Thought: Charlotte truly misreads Humbert. She imagines herself as the inappropriate and brazen one.

Bland American Charlotte frightened me. (1.20.16)

Thought: Humbert expresses very ambivalent feelings about America. Charlotte represents the parts he doesn't like – the mainstream, low-brow consumer type.

There is nothing louder than an American hotel; and, mind you, this was supposed to be a quiet, cozy, old-fashioned, homey place—"gracious living" and all that stuff. (1.29.7)

Thought: Humbert conducts an extensive study of hotels. He loves them and hates them at the same time for their tacky, contrived, and hollow qualities.

By a paradox of pictorial thought, the average low-land North-American countryside had at first seemed to me something I accepted with a shock of amused recognition because of those painted oilcloths which were imported from America in the old days to be hung above washstands in Central-European nurseries, and which fascinated a drowsy child at bed time with the rustic green views they depicted—opaque curly trees, a barn, cattle, a brook, the dull white of vague orchards in bloom, and perhaps a stone fence or hills of greenish gouache. (2.1.14)

Thought: Humbert was brought up with a distinct image of "America." Many of these images are confirmed when he actually visits the sights.

We inspected the world's largest stalagmite in a cave where three southeastern states have a family reunion [...] A granite obelisk commemorating the Battle of the Blue Licks, with old bones and Indian pottery in a museum nearby [...] The present log cabin boldly simulating the past log cabin where Lincoln was born. (2.2.4)

Thought: You can find just about anything in America. And everything is a tourist sight. It's just that most of it lacks any real historical meaning (compared to Europe).

[...] but no matter how I pleaded or stormed, I could never get her to read any other book than the so-called comic books or stories in magazines for American females. (2.3.14)

Thought: Despite being a raging nymphet, Lolita is dreadfully ordinary. Humbert often takes intellectual offense at her banality.

I also noticed that commercial fashion was changing. There was a tendency for cabins to fuse and gradually form a caravansary, and, lo […], a second story was added, and a lobby grew in, and cars were removed to a communal garage, and the motel reverted to the good old hotel. (2.16.4)

Thought: From one year to the next, America undergoes enormous change. Unlike Europe, America is constantly being updated, renovated, and improved.

"Good by-aye!" she chanted, my American sweet immortal dead love. (2.29.92)

Thought: That Lolita is American is very significant to Humbert. What qualities do Lolita and America share, for good or ill?

Plot Analysis

Classic Plot Analysis

Initial Situation
Humbert loves young girls, which is fine when he is young, but becomes complicated (and illegal) as he gets older.
From the Foreword to Humbert's memoir, we find out that Humbert died in captivity. Soon we begin reading Humbert's story, which begins by describing the childhood love that led him to his obsession with what he describes as "nymphets." A young woman named Annabel Leigh is his first love, but before gratifying his desire for her, Annabel's parents take her away. Humbert's enduring desire for young girls is established in these early chapters. He expresses a range of feelings about it – guilt, desire, rationalization – and explains that, other than nymphets, he only sleeps with prostitutes.

Conflict
Flash forward to Humbert as a grownup. He moves into the Haze household and meets Lolita, a reincarnation of Annabel.
Humbert falls in love with Lolita, the daughter of his landlady, the mediocre and lowbrow Charlotte Haze. He doesn't stand a chance of getting to Lolita as long as Mrs. Haze is around.

Complication
Humbert gets a letter from Charlotte saying basically love me and marry me or get out. He becomes worried that he will be separated from Lolita.
Humbert accepts that in order to continue being around Lolita he will have to bite the bullet and marry Charlotte. Soon after they marry, Charlotte discovers all of Humbert's dirty little secrets,

threatens to tell Lolita, but gets killed by a car, freeing up Humbert to pursue Lolita.

Climax

Humbert's takes Lolita to a hotel and has his way with her, though he is eager to let us know that she initiated the sexual encounter. (Hmm…)

Humbert finally gets what he has desired for so long. Ironically, before he swoops up Lolita from Camp Q, she has already lost her virginity to Charlie Holmes, with whom she has sex by the aptly named Lake Climax. Being the sex-filled book that it is, *Lolita* naturally has the climax of the story coincide with Humbert's own sexual gratification. What will Lolita do now that she has given herself to Humbert? As mentioned, one of the shocks of the novel is Humbert's assertion that Lolita seduces him. Once that has happened, we still wonder: Will she leave him? Will she turn him in? They end up going on a year-long trip around the United States and then shacking up in Beardsley.

Suspense

Someone is on to them.

After being together for several years, things start to go sour between Lolita and Humbert. Lolita gets a role in *The Enchanted Hunters*, the school play. Lolita and Humbert set off on another trip. This trip is quite different from the last. Humbert's levels of paranoia and jealousy are high. He suspects but cannot confirm that someone is following them and that Lolita is being unfaithful. Finally, as he has feared, Lolita disappears.

Denouement

After many years apart from Lolita, Humbert tracks her down and finds out that her abductor is none other than the Enchanted Hunters playwright, Clare Quilty.

On a second reading, you can find many clues that indicate Clare Quilty is around and possibly preying on Lolita from early on. It all adds up at the end. Now that Humbert knows who took her, he sets off to kill him.

Conclusion

Humbert murders Clare Quilty.

The long-awaited revenge is enacted. Humbert tracks Quilty down and, after reading him "the charges" in the form of a poem, shoots him several times. No one cares. Humbert goes to jail.

Booker's Seven Basic Plots Analysis: Tragedy

Anticipation Stage

Humbert loses Annabel Leigh, his childhood love, to overly protective parents. He must make up for the loss.

As a young boy, Humbert falls in love with his first nymphet. When she is taken away from him before they can consummate their love, he feels a permanent emptiness. In Lolita, he finds Annabel's reincarnation and the possibility of fulfilling his childhood lust.

Dream Stage

Humbert cannot let anything stop him from getting at Lolita.

In order to be near Lolita, Humbert must endure the bourgeois uncultured companionship of Charlotte Haze, who, as it turns out is in love with him. He is full of daydreams of how to rid himself of her and even comes close to murdering her at Hourglass Lake. He ends up marrying her just to stay near Lolita and believes that he will have to gratify himself by drugging both of the women into a stupor. Fate intervenes and he gets his wish (as well as getting off scot-free) when a car kills her, thus clearing his path to Lolita.

Frustration Stage

Though Lolita is in Humbert's clutches, things start to go wrong. She's getting some serious attitude and is possibly cheating on him. On top of that it seems like someone (a detective, perhaps?) is shadowing them on their travels.

Humbert starts to get very possessive and paranoid. Though their relationship had its troubles (like Lolita hates him and cries every night), she was still complying with his desires. Now, on their second road trip, someone in an Aztec Red Convertible is following them and Lolita is possibly in on it.

Nightmare Stage

Lolita vanishes from a hospital in Elphinstone.

Humbert loses Lolita and begins a frantic search for her. He traces back through every motel they stayed at only to find that her abductor was following them all along. Humbert is teased and tormented by the abductor's inscriptions in the motel registries.

Destruction or Death Wish Stage

Humbert is bent on revenge.

After wandering around for a few years in search of Lolita, Humbert finally receives a letter that provides clues as to her whereabouts. Almost as important as locating her is determining who abducted her. When he finds out that it is Clare Quilty, he tracks the playwright down at his family manor and shoots him like a dog. Without Lolita, Humbert has nothing, so after he shoots Quilty he drives down the wrong side of the street and just waits to be arrested.

Three Act Plot Analysis

Act I

Humbert develops a taste for young girls. He earns an education on the continent and marries Valeria in an effort to cure himself and be taken care of. They divorce. Humbert moves to United States and after some peculiar adventures and several stays in a sanitarium, moves to Ramsdale. He becomes a boarder in the Haze household, immediately falling in love with the daughter, Lolita. Desperate to stay near Lolita, Humbert marries Charlotte Haze, who conveniently dies, leaving Humbert to gratify his passion.

Act II

Humbert and Lolita begin their affair. They undertake a year-long trip around the United States, an odyssey filled with cheap motels, souvenirs, and tourist traps. They end up in Beardsley because Lolita has to go to school and Humbert must work. They live together, continuing their torrid affair, but Lolita is getting ornery. Humbert starts to become possessive. He lets her take part in the school play, which makes matters worse. After a big blow-up, Lolita proposes taking another trip. They set off.

Act III

Lolita is kidnapped. Humbert undertakes an extensive effort to find her, but is only tormented by provocative clues that prove nothing other than that her abductor is Humbert's intellectual equal. Finally after several years, and in need of money, Lolita contacts him. Humbert tracks her down, tries to win her back, finds out who she bailed with, gives her money, then leaves to kill Clare Quilty. Humbert shoots and kills Quilty and ends up in jail.

Study Questions

1. How does the Foreword influence our reading of Humbert's "memoir"? How are we meant to regard the Foreword's idea that the memoir is a "case study" with moral lessons? How do Ray's Foreword and Nabokov's Afterword speak to each other?
2. What is the effect of knowing from the beginning that the three main characters involved in the story are already dead?
3. How does Humbert draw attention to the act of writing? Why does he do this?
4. Can Humbert ever be said to "love" Lolita? Does he ever consider her a being outside of his own imagination? Is the reader ever able to see Lolita in ways that Humbert cannot?
5. Is Humbert likable? Why or why not?
6. Early on, we learn that Humbert is insane enough to have committed himself to several mental institutions, where he enjoyed misleading his psychiatrists. Is Humbert's madness an excuse or a reason for his sexual deviance? Can we trust a story told by an insane narrator?
7. From the start, Humbert sees Lolita merely as an incarnation of Annabel, even making love to her on different beaches as he tries to symbolically consummate his earlier passion. Do we believe this effort is genuine or is it just another example of his mockery of psychoanalysis?
8. Does Humbert ever succeed in escaping the past? Why is Lolita able to get past her very troubled childhood, to the extent that she can even move past the abuse inflicted on her by both Humbert and Quilty, and live a somewhat normal married life?
9. Is *Lolita* a moral story despite Nabokov's insistence in the Afterword that it is not?

10. If we believe Humbert, Lolita initiates their first sexual encounter. Yet later Humbert admits that "Lolita sobs in the night—every night, every night—the moment I feigned sleep" (2.3.18). Does what begins as a game for Lolita become a brutal and inescapable reality? Or is Humbert been lying to us from the first?
11. Does Humbert ever genuinely repent for his crimes, or is even his remorse a sham?
12. Humbert's first nymphet love is Annabel Leigh, inspired by Edgar Allan Poe's Annabel Lee (of the poem "Annabel Lee"). Aside from Annabel, can you find any other connections between *Lolita* and Poe's works?

Characters

All Characters

Humbert Humbert Character Analysis

Humbert the Hunk

Pervert and pedophile? Yes. Rapist? Yes. Murderer? Sure. Predatory, compulsive egomaniac? You betcha. Humbert is also a fearful, tortured, guilt-ridden, hand-wringing (literally, as he admits) middle-aged man. And Humbert is, above all, good looking by his accounts – indeed, with the kind of masculine handsomeness of a movie star. In his words:

I was, and still am, despite mes malheurs, *an exceptionally handsome male; slow-moving, tall, with soft dark hair and a gloomy but all the more seductive cast of demeanor.* (1.7.1)

In fact, Humbert loves his own looks almost as much as he loves Lolita's. One of his favorite characterizations is his uncanny resemblance to a Hollywood actor, with his "clean-cut jaw, muscular hand, deep sonorous voice, [and] broad shoulder" (1.11.10). He is very pleased to announce that he looks like some actor or singer Lolita has a crush on. According to Humbert, he is downright irresistible, a positive hunk whose "gloomy good looks" always get him the girl, causing Lolita to swoon, Charlotte to love him passionately and possessively, and Jean Farlow to develop a teenage crush.

Humbert the Sophisticate

Humbert is not just about looks. He's also sophisticated, intellectual, and culturally superior. An educated man, a respected if obscure scholar, and a professor of literature – he has it all. In spite of his "manly" good looks and soaring brainpower, he is shy ("horribly timid"), he

confesses, becoming nervous at the mere thought of "running into some awful indecent unpleasantness" (1.11.28).

For every expression of self-love, Humbert articulates an equal measure of self-loathing, comparing himself to "one of those inflated pale spiders" (1.11.24) who lies in wait in the middle of his sticky web. Humbert's nicknames for himself reveal the many facets of his self-image: "Humbert the Hoarse," "Humbert the Popular Butcher," "Humbert the Wounded Spider." There is, by his description, "a cesspool of rotting monsters behind his slow boyish smile" (1.11.12).

Humbert grew up in Europe, lost his mother at age three – ("picnic, lightening") (2.10) – and had a father who was "a salad of racial genes: a Swiss citizen of mixed French and Austrian descent" (1.2.1). Humbert is multilingual and highly literate – peppering his writing with French, German, and Latin phrases, legalese, and plain old sweet talk. Humbert is all about words.

Humbert's Morals, or Is There Such Thing as a Sympathetic Pedophile?
So what about Humbert's dark side? Well, he may be a self-described hottie and have a Ph.D., but he's also a self-professed madman. His world is full of illusion and fantasy, violent and transgressive impulses. He suffers from insomnia and paranoia. Even he cannot deny his two selves:

No wonder, then, that my adult life during the European period of my existence proved monstrously twofold. Overtly, I had so-called normal relationships with a number of terrestrial women [...] inly, I was consumed by hell-furnace of localized lust for every passing nymphet whom as a law-abiding poltroon I never dared approach. (1.5.8)

What makes him the pervert that he is? That's a tough one because Humbert denies us any clear response to that burning question and instead makes a mockery out of the assumption that a neat explanation is even possible. One of his biggest targets of derision is psychology and especially Freudian psychoanalysis, which assumes that one's problems as an adult could be explained by analyzing one's childhood – particularly one's childhood sexuality. Humbert both embraces and ridicules the notion that his pedophilia can be explained by the loss of his childhood love, Annabel Leigh. On the brink of making love, the two thirteen-year-olds are interrupted. Thus, according to psychoanalysis, he is always trying to relive that moment, always trying to follow through on the incomplete sexual act. (Nabokov himself professed a hatred of Freudianism).

Humbert has several stints in sanitariums (so much for healing and progress), but while there he really just enjoys messing with the doctors, who are clearly stuck on Freudian interpretations and are woefully inferior in intelligence – as is most everyone. Equipped with amateur scientific ambitions and an interest in pseudoscience, Humbert believes he has it all figured out.

Humbert's outlook is dark, coloring everything he sees. He is fundamentally cynical, assuming (or, perhaps, hoping) that others are as twisted as he is. Part of this impulse is, of course, to

make his crimes seem more natural:

Ah! Gentle drivers gliding through summer's black nights, what frolics, what twists of lust, you might see from your impeccable highways if Kumfy Kabins were suddenly drained of their pigments and became as transparent as boxes of glass! (1.27.85)

Humbert supposes and wants the reader to be as perverse as he is, to become like him so that we will be complicit and sympathetic to his acts. It's not that he *never* considers the resounding ethical compromise he is making (as some critics have said). Indeed he confesses to being "obsessed by all sorts of purely ethical doubts and fears" (1.25.1). It's just that these fears are never great enough to stem his desire; ultimately his lust is too great for him to care about the ethical repugnance of it all. But Humbert doesn't allow any simple, self-satisfied explanation. Humbert does express remorse, he does reflect on the crime and violation, and does (in the book's final pages) express something close to a moral epiphany:

Reader! What I heard was but the melody of children at play, nothing but that, and so limpid was the air within this vapor of blended voices, majestic and minute, remote and magically near, frank and divinely enigmatic—one could hear now and then, as if released, an almost articulate spurt of vivid laughter [...] I stood listening to that musical vibration from my lofty slope [...] and then I knew that the hopelessly poignant thing was not Lolita's absence from my side, but the absence of her voice from that concord. (2.36.3)

Humbert dangerously and defensively mixes beauty and morals, seeking to defend his actions by describing them as an appreciation of beauty. English author Martin Amis called him, in a wonderful summary, "without question, an honest-to-God open-and-shut sexual deviant, displaying classic ruthlessness, guile and (above all) attention to detail" (source). He is utterly cruel and sadistic; these qualities are so prominent it is shocking that they are so easily forgotten. Amidst the poetic language and the "love story," we read past the scenes Humbert's physical violence (twisting his first wife's damaged wrist and backhanding Lolita).

Humbert and Lolita: Lust Prevails

Does he love her? Well, *he* thinks so and says so plenty, but it's tough to make an argument that he could love her and exploit her as he does. Most importantly, for purposes of the memoir, Humbert *believes* he loves Lolita and has loved her all along, as he explains in his final encounter with her:

[...] and I looked and I looked at her and knew as clearly as I know I am to die, that I loved her more than anything I had ever seen or imagined on earth. (2.29.67)

How do we reconcile this expression of tenderness with his assertion that "the sensualist in me had no objection to some depravity in his prey" (1.28.2). Humbert makes it impossible.

To Humbert, Lolita is the reincarnation of Annabel Leigh, his childhood love and original nymphet. It is love (or lust) at first sight; by his account, Humbert is liberated from the past "at the moment Annabel Haze, alias Dolores Lee, alias Loleeta, had appeared to me, golden and brown, kneeling, looking up, on that shoddy veranda" (2.3.4).

At the beginning, Humbert praises his effort to maintain Lolita's purity – "Humbert Humbert tried hard to be good. Really and truly, he did" (1.5.9), but eventually he gives in to unmitigated lust. As Humbert sees it, Lolita is aware of her sexuality, putting off erotic vibes wherever they go, "aware of that glow of hers" (2.2.7). Characterizing her in this way benefits him though, in the same way calling himself an "enchanted hunter" does – it makes her partially responsible for his sexual response. During their first trip across the United States, when he hears Lolita sob every night as they lay in bed, he remains incapable of allowing sympathy to prevail over his lust – so he pretends that he is asleep.

One of Humbert's ways of keeping Lolita in his clutches with what he calls "the reformatory threat," (2.1.10), in which he threatens to send her to orphanages, reform schools, or other harsh institutions if she doesn't behave and meet his sexual demands. At one point, he menacingly asks her, "Don't you think that under the circumstances Dolores Haze had better stick to her old man?" (2.1.13). He does not hesitate to remind us (and imply to her) that as a nymphet Lolita has an expiration date; he will use up her adolescence and then move on to the next fresh nymphet. Now, Lolita does not go along unquestioningly. But the fact that she doesn't run away sooner may be an indication that she believes Humbert's propaganda and threats – that he's the best (and only) thing she's got.

At one point during their first U.S. tour, Lolita asks, as Humbert reports, "how long did I think we were going to live in stuffy cabins, doing filthy things together and never behaving like ordinary people?" (2.2.5). Humbert's increasing jealousy also makes life difficult for Lolita. The more she attempts to have a normal life, the deeper he sinks his claws into her. Sick of it all, Lolita strikes back:

She said she loathed me. She made monstrous faces at me, inflating her cheeks and producing a diabolical plopping sound […] It was a strident and hateful scene (2.14.10)

Her overt resistance to him does not last long, but she does get crafty.

Love Him or Hate Him: Humbert's Readers, Critics, and Maker
Nabokov spent a lifetime in interviews defending his resemblance to Humbert. In all descriptions of the vile protagonist, Nabokov kept a safe distance, describing Humbert as "a vain and cruel wretch who manages to appear touching" (source). Perhaps, the American literary critic Lionel Trilling says it best when he describes the reader's experience in the following way:

We find ourselves the more shocked when we realize that, in the course of reading the novel, we have come virtually to condone the violation it presents [...] we have been seduced into conniving in the violation, because we have permitted our fantasies to accept what we know to be revolting. (source)

In a sense, by continuing to read, we admit that Humbert's story *deserves* to be read, we admit that we want to know what happens, less out of a concern for Lolita than for a drive to know if he keeps her, if he gets away with it. Disgust is matched by fascination.

Critics are often divided into love-him or hate-him camps. On one side are those who admire Humbert's wit and intelligence, his passion and humor in spite of the moral abhorrence, and who focus on *Lolita's* immorality, her abject consumerism and rejection of all things literate and intelligent. On the other side we have those who give Humbert no break, taking unrelenting aim at the narcissism and tyranny of his ways and praising Lolita's bravery and resilience in the face of it.

Humbert Humbert Timeline and Summary

- 1910: First half of the year, Humbert Humbert is born in Paris, France.
- 1913: Humbert's mother is killed by lightning near Moulinet, Alpes-Maritimes.
- Summer, 1923: Humbert and Annabel Leigh's enjoy a brief love affair on the Riviera, which is thwarted by her parents.
- 1926: Annabel dies of typhoid fever on the Greek island of Corfu; Humbert begins his university studies, first in Paris, then in London.
- 1935: Humbert frequents Monique, a young Paris prostitute, then marries Valeria Zborovsky, daughter of a Polish doctor.
- Spring, 1940: Humbert sails to New York City.
- 1943: Humbert has to spend more than year in a psychiatric clinic, returns to his work, then has to go back to the hospital.
- 1944-46: Humbert joins an obscure expedition to arctic Canada as a sort of research psychologist.
- 1946-47: Soon after his return from arctic Canada, Humbert has another bout with insanity and goes back to a sanitarium.
- 1947: Humbert moves to Ramsdale, into the house of widowed Charlotte Haze and her daughter, Dolores. He is 37, she is 12 ½ years old.
- June, 1947: Humbert and Charlotte marry.
- August, 1947: Charlotte is hit by a car.
- August, 1947: Humbert comes to retrieve Lolita at Camp Q.
- August 14, 1947: Humbert leaves Camp Q with Lolita; the pair checks in to The Enchanted Hunters hotel.

- August 15, 1947: This is the day of the first sexual act between Humbert and Lolita; they begin their extensive travels all over the states.
- August, 1948: One year of travels around the US ends; they arrive in Beardsley.
- May, 1949: Humbert and Lolita leave for their second trip around the United States.
- July 5, 1949: Lolita disappears from the hospital; Humbert begins his mad search for her abductor.
- November 18, 1949: Humbert arrives in Beardsley and stays a few days.
- January, 1950: Humbert is admitted to a psychiatric clinic in Quebec again because he feels he is "losing contact with reality"; he stays until May.
- May, 1950: In a bar between Montreal and New York, Humbert meets Rita; from summer 1950 to summer 1952 he travels around and lives with her.
- 1951-52: Humbert goes to Cantrip College as a visiting lecturer.
- September 22, 1952: Humbert receives a letter from Lolita; Humbert drives to Coalmont.
- September 23, 1952: Humbert meets with Lolita, now Mrs. Richard F. Schiller.
- September, 25, 1952: Humbert kills Clare Quilty at Pavor Manor and is arrested for driving on the wrong side of the road.
- End of September to mid-November, 1952: Facing his trial, Humbert writes *Lolita*, first in a psychiatric ward, then in jail.
- November 16, 1952: Humbert dies of coronary thrombosis, "a few days before his trial was scheduled to start."
- August 5, 1955: John Ray, Jr., Ph.D. finishes his Foreword to Humbert's manuscript.

Lolita Character Analysis

Lolita at first sight:

[…] without the least warning, a blue sea-wave swelled under my heart and, from a mat in a pool of sun, half-naked, kneeling, turning about on her knees, there was my Riviera love peering at me over dark glasses. (1.10.11)

Humbert immediately regards Lolita as an incarnation of Annabel Leigh, a second chance at lust. Most importantly, the first sight of Lolita is through his eyes, as are *all* sights of her. We do not know Lolita through any perspective other than Humbert's highly subjective one – thus to talk about Lolita is to talk about Humbert's thoughts about Lolita.

It's important to remember that over the course of the six or so years represented, Lolita changes, but Humbert does not. He is already an adult and is telling the story after it has all happened. The fact that she is a fresh nymphet of twelve-and-a-half at the beginning of the story and a haggard pregnant seventeen at the end matters a lot, especially to Humbert. He keeps close watch of her nymphet quotient – remember you can't be a nymphet after fourteen. As Lolita reaches the ripe old age of fourteen, Humbert notes the changes:

Her complexion was now that of any vulgar untidy highschool girl who applies shared cosmetics with grubby fingers to an unwashed face. (2.14.2)

Lolita is a fantasy, a nymphet, and a figment of Humbert's past, a reincarnation of his lost Annabel, and a girl whose "true nature" as a nymphet, in Humbert's words, "is not human [...] but demoniac." Because "Lolita" has become synonymous with tween seductress, the reader is challenged to understand the character beyond the cultural reference – which does not reflect the fact the she is, after all, a victim and not a siren. (In an interview, Nabokov said he was "probably responsible for the odd fact that people do not name their daughters Lolita any more" (source: James Kincaid, "Lolita at Middle Age"). Do ya think?!

Lolita also changes a lot, going from the skinny-armed, freckle-faced, foul-mouthed animated girl (and icon of all nymphets) to a hugely pregnant, jaded married woman just trying to survive. The pop culture abundance and shallowness of her youth becomes a blue-collar struggle against scarcity.

But beyond Humbert's designation as "nymphet," Lolita is an ordinary North American girl-child – real name: Dolores Haze – who loves cheesy pop music, Hollywood melodramas, teeny-bopper magazines, cottage cheese, and bubble gum. She "it was to whom ads were dedicated: the ideal consumer, the subject and object of every foul poster" (2.1.7). At times she is downright boring, bratty, and gross: "There she would be, a typical kid, picking her nose" (2.1.17). Lolita curses and loves slang (words like "revolting," "super," "luscious," "goon," and "drip"), something Humbert is willing to overlook for all his love of fancy talk, Latin references, and multisyllabic words. Despite her casual air and teenage aloofness, Lolita is deeply damaged. Though she makes jokey references to having been "daisy-fresh" (1.32.33) before he defiled her, Lolita and Humbert both know that he has ruined her.

Central to Humbert's defense is that Lolita is already corrupted when he gets to her, no longer a virgin, and therefore, in his mind, fair game. Part of how he sells this image of her is not only by detailing her numerous risqué sexual experiences but also by presenting her as the ultimate shallow consumer:

[Lolita] believed, with a kind of celestial trust, any advertisement or advice that appeared in Movie Land or Screen Land—Starasil Starves Pimples, or "You better watch out if you're wearing shirttails outside your jeans, gals, because Jill says you shouldn't. If a roadside sign said: VISIT OUR GIFTSHOP—we had to visit it, had to buy its Indian curios, dolls, copper jewelry, cactus candy. (2.1.7)

Lolita, as a typical American teenager has a deep affection for the shallow and meaningless culture industry, which already implies a sort of loss of purity. That she doesn't always comply with Humbert's appetite for sex is a source of enormous frustration to him; along these lines, he describes her as "A combination of naïveté and deception, of charm and vulgarity, of blue sulks

and rosy mirth, Lolita, when she chose, could be a most exasperating brat" (2.1.7).

Ultimately, Lolita is a tough character to puzzle out because she simply does not easily fit into the victim category. She is, in spite of her treatment under Humbert, a very strong figure. It is certainly notable that she initiates the first sexual encounter – *according to him, at least*. From that moment on, she figures out how to get (almost) whatever she wants out of Humbert – new clothes, magazines, trinkets, and long vacations. She takes her victimization and uses it against him, teasing him for being a rapist and predator, even accusing him of murdering her "mummy."

But she doesn't run away until deep into their relationship, despite ample opportunity. When she does finally run away, it's into the arms of another predator, Clare Quilty. In her final encounter with Humbert, she is a disillusioned but practical young woman. She loves her husband (though isn't crazy about him as she was Clare Quilty) and bears no grudge against Humbert. She knows that what he did to her was deeply wrong – he "broke" her life, as she puts it – but finds hope in her relationship with her husband Dick and the impending birth of her baby.

It is dark to realize that as the novel begins, Lolita is already dead; but even the most astute reader would not understand that point from the Foreword, where her death (and that of her child) is announced: "Mrs. 'Richard F. Schiller' died in childbed, giving birth to a stillborn girl, on Christmas Day 1952" (Fore.3).

Lolita Timeline and Summary

- April, 1934: On the honeymoon trip of Charlotte Becker and Harold E. Haze to Veracruz, Mexico is Lolita's conception.
- January 1,1935: Dolores Haze is born in Pisky.
- 1945: The Hazes move from Pisky (Midwest) to Ramsdale (New England).
- May, 1947: Humbert moves in.
- June, 1947: Lolita goes to Camp Q.
- August, 1947: Charlotte gets hit by a car.
- August, 1947: Humbert comes to retrieve Lolita at Camp Q.
- August 14, 1947: Humbert leaves Camp Q with Lolita; the pair checks in to The Enchanted Hunters hotel.
- August 15, 1947: This is the day of the first sexual act between Humbert and Lolita; they begin their extensive travels all over the states.
- August, 1948: One year of travels around the US ends; they arrive in Beardsley at the end of August.
- May, 1949: Lolita is involved in *The Enchanted Hunters*, the school play.
- May, 1949: Humbert and Lolita leave for their second trip around the United States.
- June 27, 1949: Lolita becomes ill in Elphinstone and must check in to the hospital.
- July 5, 1949: Lolita disappears from the hospital.

- Clare Quilty takes Lolita to a dude ranch, the Duk Duk Ranch; refusing to participate in Quilty's child pornography films, Lolita is kicked out.
- Lolita drifts for two years, working in some restaurants to get by.
- Lolita meets her future husband, Dick.
- September 18, 1952: Lolita writes a letter to Humbert.
- December 25, Thursday, Christmas Day: Lolita dies in Gray Star, Alaska, "in childbed, giving birth to a stillborn child."

Clare Quilty Character Analysis

"A broad-backed man, baldish, in an oatmeal coat and dark-brown trousers" (2.18.3). Clare Quilty is Humbert's "brother" in lust, his double and worthy opponent in verbal skills. Quilty is a playwright and an admirer and maker of child pornography. Indeed, his love of young girls has already once run him into trouble with the law. By his characterization, Humbert manages to make Quilty seem even more corrupt and more perverse than him. To Humbert, Lolita must be protected from Quilty. Where Humbert "loves" and idolizes Lolita, we find out later that Quilty wants her to star in his porn movies, which is why he takes her to the Duk Duk Ranch.

Quilty fervently trails Humbert and Lolita across the United States, leaving behind a trail of provocative clues (literary references, initials, inside jokes) in motel ledgers, generally making Humbert into a (more) paranoid and jealous lunatic. Switching cars and lurking around every corner, Quilty finally "abducts" Lolita from the hospital in Elphinstone – though she is all too willing to go and has been in cahoots with him all along. Remember – she planned the itinerary for the second trip.

Even facing death, Quilty takes nothing seriously. As Humbert aims a pistol at him, he declares, "Now, *soyons raissonnables*. You will only wound me hideously and then rot in jail while I recuperate in a tropical setting" (2.35.77). He proves tough to kill, but after many shots, Humbert takes him down, reducing him to a "purple heap" (2.35.86). Shockingly, he is the only man Lolita ever really loves, or is "crazy about."

Charlotte Haze Character Analysis

This is how Humbert describes Lolita's mother, Charlotte Haze:

The poor lady was in her middle thirties, she had a shiny forehead, plucked eyebrows and quite simple but not unattractive features of a type that may be defined as a weak solution of Marlene Dietrich. (10.7)

Widow Charlotte is smart enough to impress people at a bridge gathering or a book club, but

grossly inferior by Humbert's impossibly sophisticated standards of language usage. By Humbert's description, Charlotte is a real piece of work. To him, her taste in household décor more or less says it all:

The front hall was graced with door chimes, a white-eyed wooden thingamabob of commercial Mexican origin, and that banal darling of the arty middle class, van Gogh's "Arlesienne." (1.10.4)

Her dislike of her own daughter makes her even less likable to Humbert, who can only muster any passion toward her by reminding himself that she is related to Lolita. Her death by a car swerving to miss a dog is more tragicomic than anything. The sick part is the reader is relieved for Humbert.

Annabel Leigh Character Analysis

Annabel is Humbert's childhood love and first nymphet. Humbert often references their thwarted sexual encounter (her parents took her away) and her death from typhus at an early age as having possibly made him who he is today (a pedophile). Humbert sees Lolita as a reincarnation of this original nymphet – the only way to get over Annabel.

Annabel is named after the woman in the poem "Annabel Lee" by Edgar Allan Poe. In fact, Humbert and Annabel's young love is described in phrases borrowed from Poe's poem. The part of the beginning of Chapter 1 – "Ladies and gentlemen of the jury, exhibit number one is what the seraphs, the misinformed, simple, noble-winged seraphs, envied. Look at this tangle of thorns" – refers to the poem's lines: "With a love that the winged seraphs in heaven / Coveted her and me." If you're interested in learning more about "Annabel Lee," check out Shmoop's guide to the poem.

John Ray, Jr., Ph.D. Character Analysis

Ray is the editor and author of the Foreword to Humbert's memoir. Ray is a stuffy and self-important academic who anticipates that the work will be "a case history" that will rise to become "a classic in psychiatric circles" (Fore.6). Ray offers the prudish and highly intellectual argument that all of the book's perversions will lead "unswervingly to nothing less than a moral apotheosis" (Fore.4). Not so. Through Ray, Nabokov mocks proponents of psychoanalysis.

Valeria Character Analysis

Valeria is Humbert's first wife, whom he married in an effort to cure himself from his desire for

young girls. He believes that some home-cooked meals and the routines of domestic partnership will wean him from his addictions. Valeria does, notably, remind him of young girls, as he explains:

Although I told myself I was looking merely for a soothing presence, a glorified pot-au-feu, *an animated merkin, what really attracted me to Valeria was the imitation she gave of a little girl.* (1.8.1)

She later leaves Humbert for a Russian taxi driver, which really ticks Humbert off, bringing out his violent side. Valeria later dies (in childbirth, like Lolita) in California, where she and her husband participated in some strange experiments in Pasadena.

Rita Character Analysis

Rita is a good-natured divorcée who goes along for the ride on Humbert's crazy quest around the United States to find Lolita after she has run away. Rita is basically a companion and kind-hearted alcoholic. Spending two years traveling, Humbert speaks kindly of her as "the sweetest, simplest, gentlest, dumbest Rita imaginable. In comparison to her, Valechka [Valeria] was a Schlegel and Charlotte a Hegel" (2.26.3).

Jean Farlow Character Analysis

Jean is the wife of John Harlow and friend and neighbor to the Hazes. Humbert describes her as "handsome in a carved-Indian sort of way, with a burnt sienna complexion" (1.24.1). Jean is one of the few friends Charlotte and Humbert actually spend time with, for example, at Hourglass Lake. After Charlotte's death, Jean reveals a brief crush on Humbert (and kisses him), expressing the hope that they will meet again someday. She dies of cancer at a young age.

John Farlow Character Analysis

John is the husband of Jean and friend and neighbor to the Hazes. He handles Charlotte's estate after her death. Unable to deal with the Haze legal "complications" (2.27.4), he leaves the work to an attorney named Jack Windmuller and moves to South America to live with a Spanish girl. He informs Humbert that buyers are interested in the Haze house, the sale of which allows Humbert to give Lolita a large sum of cash.

Gaston Grodin Character Analysis

A roly-poly clueless acquaintance of Humbert who teaches in the French Department at Beardsley College. He helps Humbert get a job and settle down in Beardsley. Gaston also becomes an on-and-off chess partner to Humbert and is safe to welcome into the house because he doesn't notice a thing, least of all Lolita (at one point he thinks Humbert has two daughters). His home's décor implies that his tastes run toward young men. Humbert describes Gaston as a mediocre thinker and scholar.

Dick Schiller Character Analysis

Dick is Lolita's modest, naïve, working-class husband who knows nothing of her sordid past. He's basically a really decent guy. Lolita isn't "crazy" (29.30) about him the way she was about Quilty, but he's a good guy and soon to be the father of her child. He and "Dolly" (his name for her) plan to move to Alaska and start a new life.

Mona Dahl Character Analysis

Mona is Lolita's BFF at the Beardsley School for girls. She is way too loyal for Humbert's liking because she won't out Lolita for her bad behavior. Humbert burns to know what secrets Mona holds. Humbert describes Mona as an "elegant, cold, lascivious, experienced young female" (2.9.1). At one point, she clearly develops a crush on Humbert; he's not interested.

Mrs. Pratt Character Analysis

Mrs. Pratt is the headmistress of the Beardsley School for girls. Humbert concludes that she is out of it because she thinks Lolita's eyes are blue and that Gaston is a genius. Her emphasis on the social skills (including dating and sexual proclivities) of her students over intellectual education appalls Humbert. At one point Pratt and Humbert meet to discuss Lolita's discipline problems, at which time she expresses fear about Lolita's sexual development, explaining, "She is still shuttling […] between the anal and genital zones of development" (2.11.8).

Ivor Quilty Character Analysis

The Ramsdale dentist and uncle to Clare Quilty. "A white-smocked, gray-haired man, with a crew cut and the big flat cheeks of a politician" (2.33.11). Ivor is an old friend to the Hazes. Humbert locates the nephew, Clare Quilty, by pretending he needs dental work. Ivor has no clue about the pervert his nephew is, and refers to him banally as a "rascal" (2.33.12).

Monique Character Analysis

A French prostitute who fulfills the requisite qualities of the nymphet, despite being out of the age range. Humbert sleeps with her when he lives in Paris. Their affair ends when she loses her nymphet appeal.

Charlie Holmes Character Analysis

Lolita's hook-up at Camp Q. Lolita loses her virginity with him near Lake Climax while her friend Barbara Burke keeps guard. Humbert is pleased to report that Lolita "held Charlie's mind and manners in the greatest contempt" (1.32.19). Humbert later discovers that Charlie has been killed in Korea.

Frederick Beale, Jr. Character Analysis

A man whom Humbert describes as "the fellow who eliminated my wife" (1.23.18). Beale visits Humbert shortly after the accident to explain with maps and documents how the accident was not his fault. Beale offers to pay the funeral-home expenses, which to his surprise, Humbert accepts.

Vivian Darkbloom Character Analysis

Clare Quilty's writing partner. Vivian is a "hawk-like, black-haired, strikingly tall woman" (2.18.29). Lolita tries to confuse Humbert by telling him that Vivian is a man and that Clare Quilty is a woman. Later in life, Darkbloom writes a biography of Clare Quilty, *My Cue*. Her name is an anagram for Vladimir Nabokov.

Louise Character Analysis

Charlotte's "Negro maid, a plump youngish woman" (1.10.11), whom Charlotte wants to replace with a European, full-time domestic.

Shirley Holmes Character Analysis

The director of Camp Q and mother to Charlie.

Character Roles

Protagonist *and* Antagonist
Humbert Humbert
Humbert Humbert is, much to our dismay, the main character with whom the reader identifies, but he is both hero and anti-hero, our friend for amusing us and our enemy for his moral repugnance. He himself admits to a duality and so he appropriately fills the roles of protagonist and antagonist.

Foil
Clare Quilty to Humbert Humbert
Clare Quilty is Humbert's double and shadow; they share a love of words and a lust for Lolita. He thwarts Humbert's continued relationship with Lolita. Humbert would like to see Quilty as his opposite but they have too much in common. (See "Symbols: Doubles" for a more detailed discussion.)

Guide/Mentor
Are you kidding?
Because Humbert is so crafty, no one catches on to him. There is no so-called "moral compass" in the novel and Humbert acts purely on his own desires and impulses.

Muse
Lolita
Lolita is definitely Humbert's muse, even in the traditional sense in which a muse inspires a poet to write. She is a source of inspiration poetically and erotically. She also serves as Clare Quilty's muse.

Character Clues

Names
Names tell us a lot about the characters in the novel because Humbert made the names up – all except Lolita's name, because as Ray explains in the Foreword, "her name is too closely interwound with the inmost fiber of the book to allow one to alter it" (Fore.2). The novel's first lines announce Humbert's affection for the way "Lolita" rolls off his tongue:

Lolita, light of my life, fire of my loins. My sin, my soul. Lo-lee-ta [...] she was Dolly at school. She was Dolores on the dotted line. But in my arms she was always Lolita. (1.1.1)

Of course we know that her real name is Dolores Haze, but that doesn't really have the same effect. Well, Haze isn't even her real name, it "only rhymes with the heroine's real surname" (1.1.2). Notably, the name "Dolores" contains the Latin root "dolor," which means "intense sadness" and "Haze" means, well you probably already know, but something vague, sketchy, as in "being in a haze" – in other words: out of it. Suggestively, then, Humbert refers to Lolita as "my dolorous and hazy darling" (1.11.27).

Humbert Humbert's name suggests his own duality (see his "Character Analysis" for more detail), in which trying to be good runs up against illicit desire. At the close of the memoir, Humbert explains that he has tried hard not to hurt people (though it's not exactly clear how he does this). He adds:

And I have toyed with many pseudonyms for myself before I hit on a particularly apt one. There are in my notes "Otto Otto" and "Mesmer Mesmer" and "Lumbert Lambert," but for some reason I think my choice expresses the nastiness best. (2.36.4)

Clare Quilty's name is also notable. First, it's just an odd name for a man – feminine and unfamiliar. Also, his nickname is "Cue," which is a theatrical term (as in "That's your cue to go on stage"), but it also echoes Camp Q, where Lolita loses her virginity. In prison, Humbert enjoys playing with the name "Quine the Swine. Guilty of killing Quilty" (1.8.4).

Physical Appearances

It's hard to miss how great looking Humbert thinks he is – he regularly refers to his film-worthy handsomeness and intense virility. Just as he sees Lolita's body as an object, he objectifies himself, imagining how others must be seeing him. Humbert references his own appearance throughout the novel as the kind of masculine handsomeness of a movie star. He is at once deeply narcissistic and self-loathing, on the one hand describing himself as "lanky, big-boned, woolly-chested Humbert Humbert, with thick black eyebrows" (1.11.12) and elsewhere explaining, "I was, and still am, despite *mes malheurs*, an exceptionally handsome male; slow-moving, tall, with soft dark hair and a gloomy but all the more seductive cast of demeanor" (1.7.1).

Why Humbert feels it's so important to describe his looks is unclear. He yearns to be appealing to Lolita and others – and most of all to the reader, as though his looks will make us sympathize with him, make us believe that Lolita participated willingly. Among his favorite characterizations is his remarkable resemblance to a Hollywood actor, with his "clean-cut jaw, muscular hand, deep sonorous voice, [and] broad shoulder" (1.11.10).

We know Lolita's looks matter a lot. You can't go many pages without reading one of Humbert's detailed physical descriptions, and her qualification for nymphet status depends

almost entirely on her appearance. But we can never *really* know what Lolita looks like because she is always described through Humbert's highly erotic subjective lens. When he attempts to give us any objective details about her appearance, he lapses into lust, which colors all images of her:

Only in the tritest of terms […] can I describe Lo's features: I might say her hair is auburn, and her lips as red as licked red candy, the lower one prettily plump. (1.11.13)

Not exactly an impartial collection of facts.

Speech and Language

Words are, as Humbert says at one point, his only play things. Throughout the memoir, Humbert uses language to seduce, cajole, amuse, and persuade. He also uses it to mock and intimidate. There's no denying that he has an extraordinary vocabulary on top of being multilingual, so if you haven't gotten your dictionary out yet, you should. His account is chock full of literary allusions, puns, and double entendres. He is truly a verbal trickster using every rhetorical tool available.

As much as he uses language to paint a scene, he also uses it to obscure and deceive, banking on misinterpretation – the memoir is a defense speech, after all, meant to be presented to a judge and jury. That said, everything we know of the story – even his references to the speeches and expressions of others, comes through Humbert. He has full control of the story.

There are very few direct quotations from Lolita in the text, though he does admit that he likes her slangy language in a cutesy, condescending sort of way. Ultimately, he doesn't really care what she has to say. During the entire time they live together, Lolita's direct speech is almost completely absent. Of course, he also picks and chooses what to recall of Lolita's words. Of all the characters, Quilty is the only one who earns Humbert's admiration, as Humbert explains:

[…] the tone of his brain, had affinities with my own. He mimed and mocked me. His allusions were definitely highbrow. He was well-read. He knew French. He was versed in logodaedaly and logomancy. (2.23.5)

When Humbert comes to shoot Quilty, they engage in an extended verbal duel, which, of course, Humbert wins.

Literary Devices

Symbols, Imagery, Allegory

Before going into symbols, imagery, and allegory in *Lolita*, it is important to note that Nabokov himself was very resistant, and in fact mocked, the idea that the book was full of such literary trickery. In "On A Book Entitled Lolita," an essay written one year after the book was published in France (and often included at the end of the novel), Nabokov expressed deep cynicism about the efforts of literature teachers to find deep meaning in novels, seeking to answer such questions as "What is the author's purpose?" or "What is the guy trying to do?" He claims he had "no other purpose than to get rid of that book," in other words, to purge the ideas from his head. His purpose in writing the novel, as he explains it, is to produce "aesthetic bliss." To him so-called "Literature of Ideas" is pure nonsense – "topical trash." As one critic explained it: "Mr. Nabokov explicitly denies any symbolism" (source) and in interviews he explained that he detests symbols and allegories.

Part of Nabokov's resistance to making objects deeply meaningful and figurative relates to his dislike of psychoanalysis, which posits that everything has hidden meaning. That said, there are certain images that appear and reappear throughout the novel, more motifs than hard-and-fast symbols. You will not find any symbols so strong as *The Great Gatsby*'s green light; as Freud himself (maybe) said, "Sometimes a cigar is just a cigar."

Imagery: Nymphet
"Nymphet" is Humbert's word for an attractive young girl, but he goes to great lengths to define it precisely, particularly the age range and the exact physical qualities a "girl-child" (what we might today call a "tween") must have in order to qualify for nymphet status:

Between the age limit of nine and fourteen there occurs maidens who, to certain bewitched travelers, twice or many times older than they, reveal their true nature which is not human but nymphic (that is demonaic); and these chosen creatures I propose to designate as "nymphets." (1.5.6)

Now, whether or not anyone would agree to call these girls "nymphets" remains unknown. This definition is Humbert's own, for Humbert's pleasure, and to clarify for the reader ("the jury") and his lawyer, who prompted him to write the account, exactly what constitutes the object of his lust.

Because we're dealing with a verbal trickster, it's important to pause and consider Humbert's definition. Words like "bewitched" echo his whole Enchanted Hunters theme of magic, casting spells, and fairy lands, but it also implies that the man who loves the nymphet almost cannot help himself because he is in her power, *she* is the one casting as spell and is thus in control – as Humbert suggests of Lolita when he tells us that *she* seduced him. After his initial more physical description of "nymphet," Humbert makes a further point:

What drives me insane is the twofold nature of this nymphet—of every nymphet [...] of tender dreamy childishness and a kind of eerie vulgarity. (1.11.13)

Not only does Humbert delineate "nymphet," but he also explains that one who loves nymphets must be an "artist and a madman, a creature of infinite melancholy" (1.5.6) – like him.

Imagery: The Enchanted Hunter

This phrase comes up many times during the course of the novel, and often in highly suggestive variations, such as "The Hunted Enchanters." It is first mentioned by Charlotte, who proposes that she and Humbert have a romantic little getaway at a hotel by that name. Most importantly, The Enchanted Hunters is the name of the hotel where Humbert and Lolita first have sex. Later, Clare Quilty names his play *The Enchanted Hunter* and clever Humbert doesn't make the connection – remember that man who speaks to him about Lolita on the dark porch of hotel? Quilty, gathering material. Humbert admits that he thought the name of the hotel and the name of the play was a coincidence.

The phrase echoes some of the meanings of "nymphet" because it implies that the one who hunts is "enchanted," almost under the spell of the girl being hunted. The hunter is drawn as if by a supernatural power that cannot be helped or hindered. Despite this connotation, the object of the hunt is clearly Lolita. Along these lines, Humbert often characterizes himself as a predator – like a spider or a monster, at one point saying that he prefers his prey to be moving rather than motionless. Clare Quilty is another of Lolita's hunters, following Humbert and Lolita around the country and finally snatching her up in Elphinstone.

Imagery: Cinema

Lolita is a very cinematic novel. Not only is the style highly visual, but Humbert also constantly imagines scenes unfolding as if they are up on the big screen. Lolita is also obsessed by movies, slick movie mags, and Hollywood hunks. Humbert is both compelled by Lolita's obsession and repulsed by its vulgarity. He likens himself to a virile movie actor and appreciates the comparison Lolita has drawn between himself and a "haggard lover" (1.16.7) in an ad ripped out and stuck above her bed. He is fully prepared to exploit Lolita's affection for movie-land illusions and Hollywood glamour. To Nabokov, Lolita's love of movies serves as a commentary on the larger American infatuation with movies. (And let's not forget that Quilty makes porn movies.)

The very style of the novel has a debt to the cinematic arts, as Humbert often refers to a keen awareness of being watched, referring to himself as the "glamorous lodger" with Lolita as the "modern child, an avid reader of movie magazines, an expert in dream-slow close-ups" (1.11.22). Scenes are often told in cinematic fashion with references to "Main Character [...] Time [...] Place [...] Props" (1.13.5), when Humbert has his covert gratification on the couch.

Allegory: America

America is one of the most prominent "symbols" in the book (for extended discussion see "Visions of America" under Themes). What America stands for – consumerism, kitsch culture, excessive advertising – is more of an allegory than a symbol. Humbert makes a lot of the differences between old Europe and the relatively new America, which he closely associates with Lolita and her desires. Charlotte embodies some of the worst of American tastes an impulses, in particular the bourgeois inclination to appear sophisticated by cluttering one's house with international knick-knacks. To Charlotte, Humbert is the epitome of European elegance and intelligence; by having him in her home, she hopes that some of that class will rub off on her.

Symbol: Theater

Theater plays an important symbolic role, because Lolita's involvement in it not only trains her to trick Humbert even better, but also becomes the way she gets closer to Clare Quilty, whose play, *The Enchanted Hunter*, is being staged at her school. As Humbert soon fears, perhaps Lolita's involvement in theater has trained her in the art of deception and performance:

By permitting Lolita to study acting I had, fond fool, suffered her to cultivate deceit. It now appeared that it had not been merely a matter of learning the answers to such questions as what is the basic conflict in ' Hedda Gabler' […] it was really a matter of learning how to betray me. (2.20.1)

Symbol: Doubles

Lolita is full of doubles, also knows as *doppelgängers*: Humbert and Quilty, Annabel and Lolita. (Even the name "Humbert Humbert" reflects an in inner duality.) In spite of Humbert's deep resentment of Quilty, he cannot help but admire the playwright's verbal skills. Quilty is the one person in the novel whose intelligence Humbert even remotely respects. They are bound by their perverse desire for Lolita. That Quilty follows Humbert around the United States emphasizes the sense that Quilty is a shadow figure to Humbert.

Still, Humbert and Quilty have more in common that even Humbert would like to admit. To Humbert, *Quilty* is the evil one, the depraved one, praying on Lolita. When Humbert finally confronts Quilty in the end, he announces that Lolita was his child, as though he has played a role of concerned parent and protector. In a sense, then, killing Quilty is Humbert's way of doing himself in since he knows he will go to jail where he belongs. As they fight in the end, their bodies blend together, as Humbert describes the scene: "We rolled over me. They rolled over him. We rolled over us" (2.35.55). Between Humbert and Quilty, there is a constant switching back and forth between who is the hunter and who is the hunted. They are also both "enchanted hunters" of Lolita because they are both mesmerized by her as they prey on her.

As for the Annabel and Lolita doubling, Humbert sees Lolita as Annabel's reincarnation and the cure to his life-long ache over losing Annabel. Most importantly, they are both nymphets.

Symbol: Clothing

Lolita
Shmoop Learning Guide

Clothing plays a huge symbolic role in the novel, as Humbert loves to buy clothes for Lolita. Clothes are a way for Humbert to project his fantasies onto Lolita, a way to bribe her, and a way to show his own perverse form of affection. His first mention of her includes a mention of her sock, and the first thing he does before he goes to pick up Lolita from Camp Q is buy her a bunch of clothes. His journal holds his obsessive record of what she is wears daily, "plaid shirt, blue jeans, and sneakers" (1.11.4); "rolled-up jeans" (1.11.5); "Checked frock" (1.11.10); "pretty print dress [...] ample in the skirt, tight in the bodice, short-sleeved, pink, checkered with darker pink" (1.13.5). You get the point.

Symbol: McFate

One of Humbert's favorite little catch phrases refers to the strange coincidences and convergences that Humbert experiences:

As for me, although I had long become used to a kind of secondary fate (McFate's inept secretary, so to speak) pettily interfering with the boss's magnificent plan. (27.85)

One of the most notable quirks is the reappearance of the number 342: it's the street number of the Haze home, the room number at The Enchanted Hunters, and the total number of hotels in which Humbert and Lolita stay during their travels. What the number ultimately signifies is unknown.

Setting

North America from 1947 to 1952

The main events of the story take place in America from 1947 to 1952, but there are several other settings that bear mentioning. Setting is critical to identity in the *Lolita*, as Humbert is very aware of having come from Europe, where he lived in his father's luxury hotel on the Riviera and received a top-notch education in France. Humbert refers to the first half of his life as "the European period of my existence" (1.5.8). Though he grows to despise Europe for all of its musty old history, the fact that he is from there is integral to his personality and outlook on America. His European past is also tied up with how people like bourgeois Charlotte see him: as a cosmopolitan and elegant gentleman with "old-world" manners. Likewise, Lolita's image is very tied in to America, with all of its implications of youth, shallowness, and endless consumer possibilities.

Ramsdale "the gem of an eastern state" (1.9.9) sits in stark contrast to Europe. The Haze house, where Humbert falls in love with Lolita is "a white-frame horror [...] looking dingy and old" (1.10.4). That the story takes place in North America with travels through dozens of states with all of their sights and tourist traps, motels and alluring giftshops is much more important than the smaller settings of Ramsdale and Beardsley, a town much like Ramsdale where their house bears a "dejected resemblance to the Haze home" (2.4.1). In their two trips around the U.S.,

www.shmoop.com   ©2010 Shmoop University, Inc.   72

Humbert and Lolita become all too familiar with the "Sunset Motels, U-Beam Cottages, Hillcrest Courts, Pine View Courts, Mountain View Courts, Skyline Courts, Park Plaza Courts, Green Acres, Mae's Courts" (2.1.3) – all of which are dramatically different from his father's palatial hotel on the Riviera. American motels, all interchangeable, lowbrow, and equally kitsch – provide the setting for their illicit relationship. (See "Visions of America" under Themes, for more detail.)

Above all the setting of the events is in Humbert's head. So much of what he describes is infused with his imagination. And because the story is told as a memoir through his point of view, we must realize that he filters all of the information through a perverse and yet sometimes romantic lens. As example, The Enchanted Hunters hotel is one "micro" setting that requires mentioning because of the way Humbert presents it to us. Of course, it is the setting of the "seduction" (where Humbert and Lolita first have sex):

The Park was as black as the sins it concealed—but soon after falling under the smooth spell of a nicely graded curve, the travelers became aware of a diamond glow through the mist, then a gleam of lakewater appeared–and there it was, marvelously and inexorably, under spectral trees, at the top of a graveled drive—the pale palace of the Enchanted Hunters (1.27.86)

Now, how much do we actually learn about the appearance of the hotel and how much is a muddled and fairy-tale infused fantasy on Humbert's part? The point is: when Humbert describes a setting – and here he is anticipating getting Lolita drugged and under his spell – what he "sees" is colored by desire, fantasy, paranoia, and expectation.

Narrator Point of View

First Person (Central Narrator)
With the exception of John Ray, Jr.'s academic and self-important prologue to the memoir, the novel offers one point of view, one voice, and one side of the story: that of Humbert the victimizer, whose skill with language surpasses just about any reader who comes across the novel. Humbert's superiority (to Lolita, to everyone, to the "jury" he dramatically addresses from time to time, and to us) is something that Humbert banks on.

Humbert is about as far from a reliable narrator as can be. He has had numerous stints in psychiatric clinics. One example: "A dreadful breakdown sent me to a sanitarium for more than a year; I went back to my work—only to be hospitalized again" (1.9.1). The reasons he gives for his four recorded "bouts of insanity" are "melancholia and a sense of insufferable oppression" (1.9.5), a "sexual predicament" (1.9.5), and "losing contact with reality" (2.25.5). These are what we call narrative red flags: the guy is nuts.

Still, Humbert the narrator is the ultimate manipulator and seducer, extending his skills to his

storytelling techniques. He teases the reader with hints – "a bad accident is to happen quite soon" (1.19.1) – and makes constant direct addresses to the reader, saying such things as, "Ladies and gentlemen of the jury, exhibit number one" (1.1.4) and "I want my learned readers to participate in the scene I am about to replay" (1.13.5). He also provokes the readers: "Let readers imagine" (1.15.3), wanting them to enter his mind, which itself does *a lot* of imagining. "Imagine me," he says, "I shall not exist if you do not imagine me" (1.29.5). He wants the reader to envision, invent, participate, approve, and speculate. Keep in mind that his lawyer has prompted him to write this account, which unfolds as a strange combination of self-incrimination and self-defense.

Bottom line: we cannot trust a word he says.

Genre

Autobiography (memoir), Realism, Romance, Satire and Parody, Tragedy, Mystery

Lolita is such mash-up of different genres, it's impossible to label the novel as any specific one. Just when we think it complies with one generic category, Nabokov switches and plays on all of the conventions of another, readily combining realism, romance, erotic confessional, psychological case study, and detective fiction. It's also a tragedy – after all, everyone dies in the end and the hero destroys everyone and himself. The novel's Foreword has pretentions to realism, announcing that it's a "memoir" and "case study," a sort of academic examination of abnormal psychology – but that characterization is proven wrong from the novel's opening lines, which reads like nothing so much as a romance:

Lolita, light of my life, fire of my loins. My sin, my soul. Lo-lee-ta […] she was Dolly at school. She was Dolores on the dotted line. But in my arms she was always Lolita. (1.1.1)

Despite the brutal abuse throughout, Humbert claims that he loves Lolita, almost willfully trying to make us believe we are reading a romance.

In addition to realism and romance, satire runs from beginning to end, as Nabokov derides the high moral value Ray (the writer of the Foreword) attributes to the novel – and assures the reader in the Afterword that such moral lessons are simply not there. *Lolita* is certainly not a pious condemnation of child abuse or a moral story. Nabokov resists being didactic all the way, making Ray's Foreword read like a bit of dry psychological wishful thinking. Humbert's dark humor, puns, and exaggerations all contribute to the satiric effect. Words are his only playthings, so he is going to push their possibilities to the limit, as well as do his best to amuse himself in jail (and make himself appealing to his readers).

Elements of fantasy and fairy tale take hold as Humbert and Lolita approach The Enchanted Hunters hotel. Humbert's anticipation is high, and everything is colored with a supernatural

feeling. Words like "magic," "forbid," "swoon," "dream," and "treasure," enter into Humbert's vocabulary, indicating we are entering another genre altogether – one in which instincts and desires prevail over rational decision making and reality. Notably, however, there is another shift as a sneaking paranoia begins to take hold of him immediately after he and Lolita have sex. A sense of tragedy begins to seep in:

More and more uncomfortable did Humbert feel. It was something quite special, that feeling: an oppressive hideous constraint as if I were sitting with the small ghost of somebody I had just killed. (1.32.25)

Though the "romance" commands our attention, we are also reminded throughout that we are reading a murder mystery. After all, Humbert is in jail for murder and intermittently reminds us with interjections such as:

Being a murderer with a sensational but incomplete and unorthodox memory, I cannot tell you, ladies and gentlemen, the exact day I knew with utter certainty that the red convertible was following us. (2.18.3)

The Aztec Red Convertible initiates the novel's turn toward the detective genre, as Humbert begins to accumulate clues that they are being trailed and that Lolita is not exactly being forthright. At this point in the novel, Humbert becomes both detective and criminal. Allusions to the classics of detective fiction such as Poe's "The Purloined Letter," Arthur Conan Doyle's Sherlock Holmes stories, or Agatha Christie's *A Murder Is Announced*, announce these influences.

Tone

Crafty
With Humbert as our controlling (and insane) narrator, the tone comes across as sly, superior, darkly comic, and intellectual, alternating between bemused weariness and sweeping romanticism. With very few emotional outbursts, Humbert's narrative remains cool and detached, amused in spite of itself. Humbert expresses both shame and bravado (I got her! I'm such a pig – my bad. But I'm the man!).

His constant addresses to the reader are difficult to take seriously, given that they are often followed by detailed exemplifications of his vile behavior. These addresses become failed efforts to set a tone of sympathy, to draw the reader into his point of view and thus to pull back our attention from the juicy story and consider the profoundly disturbing moral implications of what we are reading. In other words, if we *like* him or *are like* him, we won't condemn him; he thus uses tone to seduce us, make us comfortable, saying sit back and enjoy the ride. Humbert's dark humor and wit also serve as part of the narrative's smoke and mirrors, seeking to erase

some of the horror trivializing the subject matter by offering jokes where shock may be more readily expected.

Writing Style

Poetic and Pretentious ("Fancy")

For a book known for being very risqué, *Lolita* has no four-letter words or graphic sex; that's because of Humbert's style, which combines the lyrical and clinical, the poetic and the academic, evoking Edgar Allan Poe and then height-charts, road maps, post cards, "evidence" and exhibits. Our narrator, Humbert, riddles the narrative with wordplay and wry observations of American culture, while his black humor provides an effective counterpoint to the pathos of the tragic plot.

The novel's humorous and ornate style is the result of double entendres, multilingual puns, anagrams, and coinages. The style is also highly visual; Humbert often compels the reader to see what he describes. [What do you expect from someone who says in the opening chapter "You can always count on a murderer for a fancy prose style" (1.1.3)?] In this sense, the American love of cinema (and Humbert's feeling that he has screen-star virility) seeps into the style of the novel.

Like the novel's genre, style often changes to serve Humbert's purpose. Half-way through the novel, he reminds us:

My lawyer has suggested I give a clear, frank account of the itinerary [Lolita and I] followed, and I suppose I have reached here a point where I cannot avoid that chore. (2.1.17)

Despite claiming an inconvenience at having to relate the details, Humbert clearly relishes it. He is at his best when he lapses into the lyrical language of enchantment – that's when he gets really fancy. Speaking of a shopping trip for Lolita, Humbert muses:

Lifesize plastic figures of snug-nosed children with dun-colored, greenish, brown-dotted, faunish faces floated around me. I realized I was the only shopper in that rather eerie place where I moved about fishlike, in a glaucous aquarium. I sensed strange thoughts. (1.25.7)

What's Up With the Title?

The name "Lolita" is everything, as Humbert indicates in the book's opening lines. It's poetry, a religious incantation, and an erotic gratification. Importantly, we know from the novel's Foreword that Lolita's name is the only one that has *not* been changed, which is interesting because she is really the only "innocent" to protect, as they say. But since the sound of her name – and Humbert's affection for the way it rolls off his tongue ("Lo-lee-ta") – is so integral to

the attraction, the name goes unchanged. As Ray explains, "her name is too closely interwound with the inmost fiber of the book to allow one to alter it" (Fore.2). The novel would be quite different if it were titled *Dolores Haze*, which is Lolita's real name.

As the Foreword indicates, Humbert's manuscript originally had the title, *Lolita, or the Confessions of a White Widowed Male*. The book's title may be *Lolita*, but it really should be *Humbert's Lolita*, because we never get a chance to hear from her at all. On that note, some critics differentiate "Dolores" (a character we never actually meet) from "Lolita," who is a projection of Humbert's fantasy. (For more discussion of names, see "Character Clues.")

What's Up With the Ending?

On the one hand, the ending of *Lolita* is open-and-shut: everyone is dead. On the other hand, the conclusion is complicated by the fact that we only know everyone's fate by going back and re-reading John Ray, Jr.'s Foreword. In other words, the end is told at the beginning when Ray announces that "Humbert Humbert," the author of *Lolita, or the Confessions of a White Widowed Male* has "died in legal captivity, of coronary thrombosis [...] a few days before his trial was scheduled to start" (Fore.1). Some paragraphs later, he relates what happened to Rita, Vivian Darkbloom, and most importantly, Mrs. "Richard F. Schiller," whom at that point we have no way of knowing is Lolita; we only know that she "died in childbed, giving birth to a stillborn girl on Christmas Day 1952, in Gray Star, a settlement in the remotest Northwest" (Fore.3). By putting the end at the beginning, Nabokov gets to resolve everyone's story and leave the memoir itself feeling really open-ended.

For its part, Humbert's "memoir" concludes with Humbert in prison. It has taken him 56 days to write the story. He comes across as rather pleased at having finished, announcing, "This then is my story" (2.36.4). Most important for Humbert is that finishing the memoir provides some sort of relief. After all, he does call it a "confession," and refers to it as such several times. He expresses concern about hurting the people who appeared in the story, so he changes their names and requests that the story not be published until everyone has died.

Do we believe that he really feels all of this guilt, compassion, and concern? His story has made him very difficult to trust. The final lines are deeply emotional, but also didactic (teacher-y), as he offers advice to Lolita about how to live a decent life. What's odd is that he gives all of these suggestions knowing that she would be dead and thus never actually read them.

Did You Know?

Trivia

- There's a annotated version of the novel to let you know what every line refers to! It's almost twice as long as the book, clocking in at 544 pages. (Source)
- On Urban Dictionary everyone has his or her own definition of Lolita, though some seem not to have read the book – look t-shirts for sale!
- Lolita Fashion. The name says it all.

Steaminess Rating

R, or even X

It's tough to give this novel a rating because it has no overt scenes of sexuality. Sexual acts are described in the vaguest of ways, often with Latin terms standing in for clear depiction. If you look up the Latin words in a dictionary and read really closely, you do get a sense of the deepness of Humbert's perversions as well as the various sex acts in which he and Lolita engage.

The novel warrants an R at the very least for its illicit subject matter (though the author of the Foreword would disagree, claiming that sexual scenes are "functional" and not "sensuous," moral and not arousing). The novel includes rape, incest, pornography, prostitution, and sex of all kinds. According to IMDb.com, the 1962 movie version did not have a rating, but it included warnings that "A girl seduces her stepfather to have sex with her." The 1997 version was rated R.

Allusions and Cultural References

Historical Figures

- King Akhenaten (1.5.8)
- Catullus (1.15.3)
- Hitler (2.8.11)
- James I (1.5.8)
- Queen Nefertiti (1.5.8)

Biblical Characters

- Eve (1.5.9)
- Lilith (1.5.9)

Musical References

- *Carmen* (1.13.14)
- Tchaikovsky (2.6.1)

Artists

- Aubrey Beardsley (2.23.5)
- Nijinsky (2.6.1)
- Reginald Marsh (2.12.4)

Literary Figures and Literary References

- Annabel Leigh (1.2.3) Humbert Humbert's first love is named after the woman in the poem "Annabel Lee" by Edgar Allan Poe. In fact, their young love is described in phrases borrowed from Poe's poem. The part of the beginning of Chapter 1 – "Ladies and gentlemen of the jury, exhibit number one is what the seraphs, the misinformed, simple, noble-winged seraphs, envied. Look at this tangle of thorns" – refers to the poem's lines: "With a love that the winged seraphs in heaven /Coveted her and me."
- *Arabian Nights* (2.3.14)
- Aristophanes (2.23.5)
- Baker's *Dramatic Technique* (2.11.32)
- Charles Baudelaire (2.2.11)
- Beatrice (1.5.8; 1.25.4)
- Remy Belleau (1.11.18)
- Bluebeard (2.22.15)
- Robert Browning (1.27.88)
- Chateaubriand (2.1.2)
- Anton Chekhov, *Cherry Orchard* (2.20.1)
- Agatha Christie (1.8.8)

- Samuel Taylor Coleridge (2.23.6)
- Dante (1.5.8; 1.25.4)
- Charles Dickens (1.8.8)
- Fyodor Dostoevsky (1.17.2)
- Norman Douglas (2.6.1)
- *The Emperor's New Clothes* (2.13: 1)
- Freud (2.23.6)
- John Galsworthy (2.2.2)
- André Gide (2.6.1)
- *A Girl of the Limberlost* (2.3.14)
- Gustave Flaubert (2.1.2)
- *Hansel and Gretel* (2.13.1)
- Henrik Ibsen, *Hedda Gabler* (2.20.1)
- Hegel (2.26.3)
- Peter Hurd (2.12.4)
- James Joyce (Fore.4): Referenced in the following passage: "the monumental decision rendered December 6, 1933 by Hon. John M. Woolsey in regard to another, considerably more outspoken book" [Fore.4]: the decision in the case United States v. One Book Called *Ulysses*, in which Woolsey ruled that James Joyce's novel was not obscene and could be sold in the United States.)
- *King Lear* (2.27.3)
- Rudyard Kipling (2.35.36)
- Laureen (1.5.8)
- *Little Women* (2.3.14)
- Maeterlinck (2.35.77)
- Moliere (2.23.6)
- Petrarch (1.5.8)
- Edgar Allan Poe (1.25.4)
- Polonius, a character in *Hamlet* (2.1.11)
- Marcel Proust (2.6.1)
- Pierre de Ronsard (1.11.18)
- Sade's *Justine* (2.29.61; 2.35.54)
- *The Sleeping Beauty* (2.13.1)
- William Shakespeare, *The Taming of the Shrew* (2.9.2)
- Ivan Turgenev (2.33.3)
- Uncle Tom, a character in *Uncle Tom's Cabin* (1.27.95)
- Friedrich von Schlegel (2.26.3)
- Frederick Waugh (2.12.4)
- Grant Wood (2.12.4)

Best of the Web

Movie or TV Productions

Lolita, 1962
http://www.imdb.com/title/tt0056193/
Stanley Kubrick (director of _The Shining_ and other greats) directed _Lolita_ in the 1962. It starred James Mason and Sue Lyon, with Peter Sellers as a super-freaky Clare Quilty. Nabokov wrote the screenplay, which was nominated for an academy award. His screenplay (dated Summer 1960 and revised December 1973) was published by McGraw-Hill in 1974.

Lolita, 1997
http://www.imdb.com/title/tt0119558/
The movie was made again in 1997 starring Jeremy Irons and directed by Adrian Lyne. This version was given mixed reviews by critics and was delayed for over a year because of its controversial subject matter.

Historical Documents

Herald Tribune Interview (1962)
http://writerinterviews.blogspot.com/2008/03/vladimir-nabokov.html
One of Nabokov's earliest interviews on _Lolita_.

Playboy Interview (1964)
http://kulichki.com/moshkow/NABOKOW/Inter03.txt
A good discussion of the first movie version.

The Sunday Times Interview (1969)
http://www.kulichki.ru/moshkow/NABOKOW/Inter12.txt
A clever and witty exchange with the author.

Original Review in the _NY Times_ (1958)
http://www.nytimes.com/books/97/03/02/lifetimes/nab-r-booksoftimes.html
A famous review by Orville Prescott.

Original Review in the _National Review_ (1958)
http://www.nationalreview.com/flashback/flashback200604200600.asp
"A Lance into Cotton Wool," by Frank S. Meyer. This review ran in the Nov. 22, 1958, issue of _National Review_.

"Think Tank; 'Lolita' Turns 40, Still Arguing for A Right to Exist"
http://www.nytimes.com/1998/08/01/movies/think-tank-lolita-turns-40-still-arguing-for-a-right-to-exist.html?pagewanted=1

Outrage over Adrian Lyne's film version of the novel (August 1, 1998).

"Vintage Review: Even in 1958, 'Lolita' was Esthetic Bliss"
http://latimesblogs.latimes.com/jacketcopy/2009/11/vintage-book-review-even-in-1958-lolita-losa
ngelestimes.html
Retrospective Review of Lolita in the *Los Angeles Times* (2009)

The Complete Review
http://www.complete-review.com/reviews/nabokovv/lolita1.htm#summaries
A website with snippets of dozens of original reviews.

Why Nabokov Detests Freud
http://www.nytimes.com/books/97/03/02/lifetimes/nab-v-freud.html
Excerpts from interviews with Nabokov.

NY Times Topic Page
http://topics.nytimes.com/topics/reference/timestopics/people/n/vladimir_nabokov/index.html
Includes links to everything the *NY Times* has written on Nabokov.

Video
1962 Movie Trailer
http://www.youtube.com/watch?v=gGGdV7PAEuw
Original trailer of Stanley Kubrick's *Lolita* (1962).

1997 Movie Clip
http://www.youtube.com/watch?v=8D_Bo0UFxq4&feature=related
Clip from the opening of Adrian Lyne's *Lolita* (1997).

Lolita Fashion
http://www.youtube.com/watch?v=HSYR34g9yGM&feature=related
Clip of a Gothic Lolita Fashion Show.

Author Interview
http://www.youtube.com/watch?v=Ldpj_5JNFoA
Nabokov discusses *Lolita*.

Audio
Nabokov Interview
http://www.bbc.co.uk/bbcfour/audiointerviews/profilepages/nabokovv1.shtml
Clips of a 1969 BBC interview with Nabokov.

At 50, 'Lolita' is Aging Well
http://www.npr.org/templates/story/story.php?storyId=4853591

A 2005 All Things Considered episode on Lolita, from NPR.

'Lolita' Turns 50
http://www.npr.org/templates/story/story.php?storyId=4848976
More from NPR: "Madeleine Brand explores how Vladimir Nabokov's groundbreaking novel about forbidden desire has rippled out into American culture."

50 Years Later, 'Lolita' Still Seduces Readers
http://www.npr.org/templates/story/story.php?storyId=4846479
This two-part special from NPR also includes lots of other great audio links, including Nabokov reading from *Lolita* and clips of actor Jeremy Irons's reading of the audio book.

Images

Lolita Fashion
http://newyork.timeout.com/articles/i-new-york/68741/lolita-fashion#ixzz0csZSIKjC
Lolita fashion, described as "The hottest fashion out of Japan turns adults into dollies – re-creating the look in New York just takes a little dress-up."

Gothic Lolita
http://www.morbidoutlook.com/fashion/articles/2002_07_gothiclolita.html
Many links to other sites that will help you fully establish your *Gothic Lolita* image.

Road Trip
http://www.dezimmer.net/LolitaUSA/LoUSpre.htm
An itinerary of Humbert and Lolita's trips around the United States.

Book Covers
http://www.librarything.com/work/913/covers/
Over 175 different covers for the novel

The Original
http://www.fedpo.com/BookDetail.php?bk=283
Photos of the first editions of *Lolita*.

The Author
http://www.themodernword.com/scriptorium/nabokov.jpg
A photo of Nabokov.